Michaela Strauss
Understanding Children's Drawings

Michaela Strauss

Understanding Children's Drawings

Tracing the Path of Incarnation

with Notes on the Study of Man
by Wolfgang Schad

translated by Pauline Wehrle

RUDOLF STEINER PRESS

Rudolf Steiner Press
Hillside House, The Square
Forest Row, RH18 5ES

www.rudolfsteinerpress.com

Revised edition 2007
First edition, Rudolf Steiner Press 1978; reprinted 1988

Originally published in German under the title *Von der Zeichensprache des kleinen Kindes* by Verlag Freies Geistesleben, Stuttgart, 1978

A catalogue record for this book is available from the British Library

ISBN 978 1 85584 199 4

Cover featuring a painting by a five-year-old girl
Printed and bound by EGEDSA, Sabadell

Contents

Preface to the Revised Edition 7
 (Margret Costantini)

Preface to the First Edition 9
 (Ernst Weißert)

How this Book Arose 11

The Forces at Work in the Drawing of
Pre-school Age Children 15

I. LINE AND MOVEMENT

Components of Pre-school Age Children's
Drawings 23

The Picture of Man and the Picture
of the Tree 37

The Human Being and the House 51

Head-and-Feet People –
Head-and-Limb People 59

II. FROM LINE TO SURFACE

Colour as the Medium of Soul Expression . . . 63

III. FROM SYMBOL TO ILLUSTRATION

Graphic-illustrative Compositions 71

Notes on the Study of Man 85
 (Wolfgang Schad)

Bibliography 95

Girl, 4 years 6 months

Preface to the Revised Edition

Since its first appearance this book has stimulated many teachers and parents to look at their children's drawings with new interest; it has enabled them to understand what they see and really enter into the process taking place in drawings of small children in the course of their development during their first seven years. This was the first publication to attempt to introduce into the sphere of the work of Waldorf education the phenomenon of children's drawings, in their connection with the principles of Rudolf Steiner's anthropology. For a long time now this has been a basic element in the educational field, providing both a first orientation and at the same time encouragement to teachers to make their own observations and proceed with further discoveries. This not least by way of the most impressive and comprehensive collection of drawings made over a long period of time.

In addition to these children's drawings a great deal of literature has meantime been available from the direction of psychology, education, art or ethnology. Themes to do with psychological matters began to appear already in the second half of the nineteenth century, when Herbert Spencer, in his publication *Education* (1861) was one of the first people to undertake an analysis of children's drawings.

A special interest in this topic, however, came from artists. In their search for what was 'universal', renowned artists such as Vassily Kandinsky, Gabriele Münter, Paul Klee, Pablo Picasso, Joan Miró and many others, were so impressed by how natural and original these children's drawings were that they were inspired by them in their own work. (In 1995 a very interesting exhibition took place in Munich on this theme.)

Hanns Strauss (1883-1946) was both a painter and an art teacher. These children's drawings became the most important research theme of his life, because they revealed to him the path of incarnation. He collected thousands of children's drawings, and compared and evaluated them. His interest in the development of the young child, with these pictures to help him, was particularly stimulated by studying Rudolf Steiner's *Study of Man*. After the early death of Hanns Strauss his daughter Michaela Strauss continued the collection made by her father, making them available for the work of education in the future. With the support of others she worked her way into the theme and brought the research work on these children's drawings to the point where this book could arise.

Many people with a similar interest gathered around Michaela Strauss. These people had for many years been doing further work on these children's drawings in connection with Rudolf Steiner's *Study of Man*, so as to learn to understand children's drawings better and better, and to be able to pass on their findings in lectures and seminars. One of the individuals in this working group was Klara Hattermann. Through her the children's drawings became an integral part of the training centres for Waldorf teachers and an established and important part of the teacher training. Together with Michaela Strauss she founded a working group for the research of children's drawings in Hanover, which I was able to continue after Frau Hattermann retired.

Even before the book appeared in Germany in 1976 (in Britain in 1978) Michaela Strauss had realized, from comparing pictures drawn by children at different periods of time, that in pictures drawn before the Second World War children had made their 'statements' much more clearly than in present day pictures. This made her ask whether this could be caused by the increasingly occurring phenomenon of nerviness and over-stimulation.

Several years have passed since then. Observations made in recent times (especially in cities) can only emphasize that the 'classic course of development' seen in pictures drawn during the first seven years of life is no longer seen in all children's drawings, especially in those drawn during the pre-school years. There may be various reasons for this. Certainly the still massive over-stimulation of the present time has a lot to do with it. Over and above this is the fact that children no longer have so much time any more in which they can, without any *pressure from outside*, do their drawings in a certain calm and carefree way, or they are told at much too early an age to draw things unsuitable for their stage of development. Something of the child's own being, a universal quality, is lost. The child can no longer, out of itself, as it unconsciously draws its way through the 'leaving behind of its traces' through the discovery of colour, and on to drawing out of its imagination to copying what it sees outside,

acquire the firm basis upon which school lessons can be built further.

For those teachers who are interested in working with children's drawings and want to read from them the unfolding path of child development, it is of great benefit that this book of Michaela Strauss' has become available again in this essentially unaltered new edition. It not only shows the phenomenon of children's drawing, but shows us enough to encourage us to be active ourselves in observing and studying in greater detail the general path of development throughout the drawings, as well as the separate drawings of individual children, and to work further on it ourselves through our own observations in this field. This could contribute to our getting a bit nearer to a solution of the still innumerable riddles hidden in children's drawings.

Margret Costantini, July 2007

Preface to the First Edition

The Pedagogical Research Centre of the Bund der Freien Waldorfschulen (Rudolf Steiner Schools Fellowship in Germany) is pleased to be able to present Michaela Strauss' book. Its publication awakens many memories in the older teachers of the Waldorf School Movement. It was in the middle thirties, at the time when the Waldorf Schools were seriously threatened politically, that we first heard of our colleague Hanns Strauss' efforts to interpret the creative work of early childhood. We were interested to see his collection of children's drawings and paintings growing. During the following difficult years, actually during the early years of the closing of the schools,* Strauss went on lecture tours to different groups of the 'Fellowship for Freedom in Education (Waldorf School Fellowship)' in Germany. We have a vivid picture of the man, serious and to the point. He had lived in Munich for many years as a painter and was connected with Waldorf pedagogy from 1923 onwards.

In the twenties, when we were young people, our attention was attracted by the task that Rudolf Steiner gave his first college of teachers: to do research as well as teach and also to use this knowledge to 'educate' the public. In our series 'Menschenkunde und Erziehung' ('study of man and education') we can find many examples of such scientific activity. So the work of Hanns Strauss concerned us from an early date, but un-

fortunately owing to his illness and early death in October 1946 the publication of his material was postponed for decades. We are grateful that his daughter, our colleague Michaela Strauss, enabled the work to be carried on and completed. What she has now achieved is also thanks to those colleagues, who, like for instance Dr Erich Schwebsch, wanted it to be continued after Strauss' death for the sake of the Waldorf Movement.

Rudolf Steiner's concept of man requires a fundamentally new study of the first seven years of life; he pointed out that future tasks for our consciousness and stimuli for social forms of the future are to be found in it. Think of the mysterious early stages of incarnation; the trinity of learning to walk, speak and think, the beginning of life experience and of creative activity. The intimate concern with the development and education in early childhood right from the beginning of Waldorf pedagogy has given our school movement a quite distinct character.

We look on Michaela Strauss's book as an important pioneer work, and we hope that it will strengthen observation, understanding and love for the being of the child both in the parental home and in kindergartens. This book will therefore be of immediate importance, too, for the rapidly spreading work of Waldorf Kindergartens.

Ernst Weissert

---

* Waldorf Schools in Germany and Austria were closed by the Nazis. (Ed.)

Girl, 5 years
6 months

How this Book Arose

This book is based on material which has been collected over the course of more than forty years. At the end of the 1920s Hanns Strauss (1883-1946) gathered together the first material for this work. He was not concerned with aesthetic points of view but with the child's spontaneous efforts at drawing without any influence from adults. His interest in children's early drawings was awakened by their lively, dynamic style. As painter and art teacher his enthusiasm was fired by the carefree freshness of this testimony of childhood.

To begin with, the basis of this collection consisted of drawings done by children of friends of his. But the material was soon increased by a wealth of drawings from the most varied connections. So the mainstay of this collection is a series of pictures showing the continuous artistic development of particular children besides a large number of pictures from families and kindergartens. In an early article in 1932* Hanns Strauss describes his attitude to the phenomenon of children's drawings: 'the position of grown-ups who find themselves faced with drawings from early childhood is this. They open a book in which are written mysterious signs of an ancient power of creation rejuvenated in the child.' On the track of these mysteries the child has drawn a great number of curves and loops ... 'for an intellectual understanding alone is not enough, but the whole of the human being must imitate it with its organism of movement and it must be completely one with it in feeling, if the rhythms and forms are to become an experience that grasps the character of the phenomena'.

The mountain of drawings grew as, time and again, the collector's enthusiasm was aroused. So Hanns Strauss compiled hundreds of pages, until certain typical characteristics showed up more and more clearly and a phenomenological one could substitute the method of summary collecting.

In the search for indications that might contribute to the understanding of the problems, Hanns Strauss encountered Britsch-Kornmann's, Kienzle's and Hartlaub's expositions on pedagogy and psychology through art. These helped him to see the drawing of young children in broader connections. Interpretations reached by the art teachers Grözinger and R. Meyer appeared only after his death.

Hanns Strauss left behind a collection of about 6,000 pictures besides aphoristically written notes. They form the basis of this book. The constant additions to the picture collection, as well as the recent increase in literature on this theme, forced me to make a completely new start with the choice of illustrations and text. The stages of development can be seen with greater and greater clarity. In this book a direction is taken which enables many things that appeared meaningless to become a key for the understanding of

* For reference see bibliography, page 95.

the incarnating human being, when seen against the background of Rudolf Steiner's knowledge of man. This conception was the basis of Hanns Strauss' notes, and constituted the main thread of his research. The anthropological notes by Wolfgang Schad in the appendix explain the close connections existing between the activity of painting and drawing and the stages of the child's bodily growth. Originally the collection only comprised drawings from Europe. Recently, however, it was possible to include pictures from outside Europe. So it becomes apparent that all children – today as well as one and a half generations ago – find their way to the same formulations in their *hieroglyphs* according to their stage of development. In the same way as the first babbling is unconnected with particular ethnic languages, this first picture writing is also universally human. In this early period of the first seven years the language of symbols is the same the whole world over.

The wealth of available material makes it possible for the various stages expressed by the child in drawings to be clearly highlighted. The examples that have been chosen demonstrate the development of a normal child. They have been picked from various courses of development of particular children and present in this way an essence of the whole collection.

Not every child expresses his developmental process as precisely as it has been possible to do in this collection. Nevertheless, with careful study of the drawings of any child we will find the essential elements. Some stages, perhaps, are only indicated, whilst others appear very distinctly. It would go beyond the range of this book to dwell on deviating symptoms (e.g. retarding or regressive elements).

A comparison of the drawings that originated before the Second World War with the most recent ones shows that compared with nowadays the children at that time drew their messages more clearly. The phenomena have remained the same, but children's unconscious perception of the laws of development of their own being – which are mirrored in their drawings – appears to have become weaker. Should this fact be seen in connection with the nervousness and overstimulation of today?

This book has been arranged so that to begin with the reader is introduced to the subject gently. We are made acquainted with the main theme by way of open-minded observation of young children's drawings. We accompany the child's activity through the stages of the first seven years. Children show us in their drawings what it is that occupies them. Let them speak for themselves through their drawings and unveil the depths that urge them to express themselves the way they do. The text is only meant as an orientation for the deciphering of the 'clues of the mystery'. One will be able to do justice to the trains of thought if one practises science in the Goethean sense. If an effort at awareness* is given priority in the act of observation, then many an objection to the effect that postulates are being presented here will vanish away.

Discussions about pre-school age problems have brought the development of the young child into the limelight in recent years. We hope the

---

* 'In science all depends on what one calls an aperçu, a becoming aware of what is actually at the root of the observations. And an awareness of this kind is infinitely fruitful.'
    Goethe, *History of the Theory of Colour.*

present publication represents a further contribution for parents and educators on this theme. If the present exposition of children's pictures succeeds in contributing to an understanding of the child, if it is a help to people engaged in the care of children – and a joy to everyone who loves children – then the purpose of this book will have been achieved in the best possible way.

I would like to take this opportunity of thanking everybody who has contributed to the making of this book: My thanks go to the parents who collected their children's drawings, and to Mrs Klara Hattermann as the representative of everyone who was stimulated by Hanns Strauss' ideas to gather material within the Waldorf Kindergarten Movement. My thanks are due to the Pedagogical Research Centre of the Waldorf School Fellowship who assisted the present work with a research grant. I would like to thank my friends for all their help, especially Mrs. Erika Sprenger-Steinmüller, who is closely associated with the progress of this book. And my thanks go to Walther Roggenkamp for his help with the artistic presentation.

Michaela Strauss

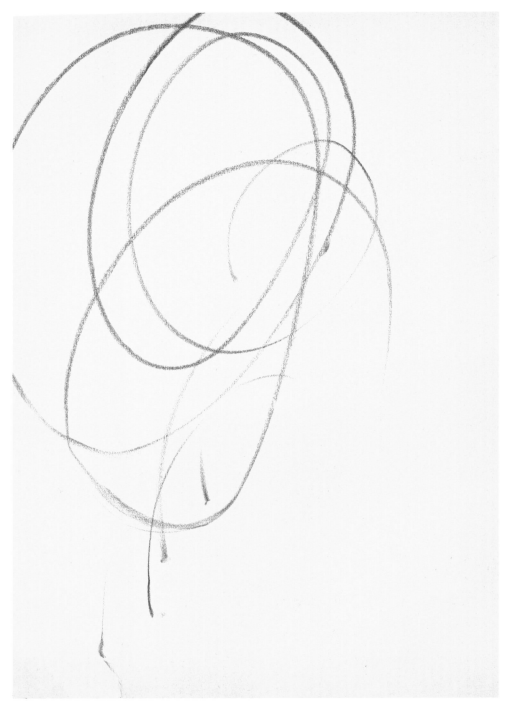

Girl, 2 years 8 months

The Forces at Work in the Drawing of Pre-school Age Children

In the search for the forces which motivate the drawing of pre-school age children, let us follow the creative process without any preconceptions. Children often start drawing before the second year. Prior to doing this they experiment timidly with the paper. Out of the liveliness of their own organism and in imitation of the grown-ups they grasp a chalk. So their first attempt at drawing is a 'written down' scribble. Imitation can trigger it off, it opens the floodgates and a torrent of creation bursts forth.

Children begin by creating big loops that come from distant spaces; these constitute the overture in which all the main themes are already intoned. In their drawings children reveal realms with which at this early age they are still intimately connected.

Long before the child does pictorial illustrations, lines are visible on the paper which are not related to objects. There appear flowing rhythms, which gradually materialize as a symbolical language of forms. Illustrative elements enter only gradually into these compositions. The drawings of this early stage show in an impressive way how intensely the child lives till the third year in movement and rhythm. The chalk reveals the child writing dancingly in space; choreographies – lines of rhythmic-dynamic life. They are processes, which condense out of primeval movement and finally come to rest in symbolical, geometrical forms.

The intensity of the creative process is expressed in the extraordinarily living 'hand-writing' of this age, in sweeping curves, ribbon-like patterns, repetitive structures, punctuated strokes and acute and obtuse angles. The movement often goes further than the paper or starts beyond the edge of the page. The loops could get bigger and bigger and sometimes they leave their traces on the given piece of paper as though by mere chance (opposite).

The quality of the stroke of these young artists lets us take a direct part in the process of formation. Varying tempi in the course of movement are expressed in the liveliness of the lines; full, broad, soft strokes side by side with a quick, barely visible touch turn these compositions into a musical experience. One can read all the nuances in the stroke, from the tenderest pizzicato to the broadest crescendo. 'Scribbles are letters that children write to themselves, an understanding with themselves ...' (W. Grözinger). They have the character of drawn 'records', and are not meant for other people. The child's interest in what it has just produced appears to be exhausted when the impulse has run its course.

The explanation of these earliest drawings has to remain unsatisfactory if one does not look far enough, if one merely wants to look at the results of this activity as an expression of what is given in the anatomical basis of the child's body, the muscles and joints. Can the variety of forms in the dynamic of young children's writing, 'stroke-scribbles', 'loop-scribbles' and 'circle-scribbles' (H. Meyers) really be explained out of the mechanics of function only? The instrument of the body and its given functions are of course already there before the child takes up the chalk. Yet impulses are obviously at work building up and forming the whole organism. We must widen our scope to include deeper layers of life-processes and formative-processes (see Notes on the Study of Man). Where do we perhaps find similar formations in greater connections? Is it misleading if, in considering these first loops drawn by children, associations with the rhythmic movements in the cosmos force themselves upon us? Do not these curves remind us of the looping orbits of the planets (opposite), and don't we find a form-relationship with the flowing rhythms of fluids (adjacent)?

Theodor Schwenk shows how structured shapes crystallize out of flowing forms that arise out of primeval movement, and he also shows how the shaping element becomes part of form-creating movement. By means of experiment he shows formative processes that underlie the most varied organs and that determine the structuring of muscles and bones.

In the child's drawing the shape appears to form itself out of processes governed by the laws of growth. Linear structures of movement are consolidated and become the first presentation of the human being. These have a completely embryonic effect and remind one of an early differentiation of brain and spinal cord.

Parallels can be seen between young children's drawings and the evidence of early history of art and culture. It is quite clear that the child's symbolic expressions are also to be seen in the finds

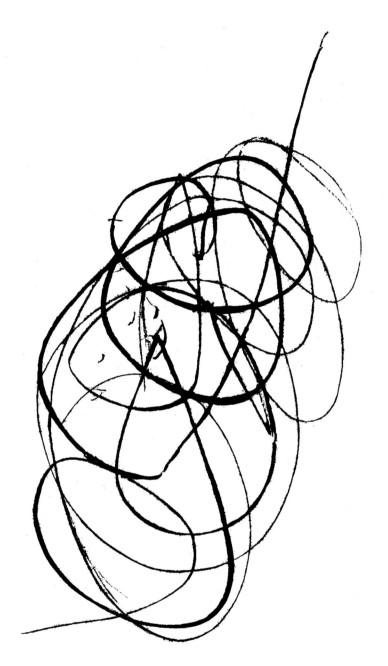

Boy, 2 years 4 months

Boy, 2 years 3 months

of earlier cultures. Are we dealing with a language of symbols that is at the root of everything that is coming into being? In the smeared lines at Pech-Merle (below) or Owens Valley (right) are we not encountering a 'scribbling stage' of humanity? Are structures being condensed out of a sea of formative forces that are related to those, which the child draws? The roots of ornamentation belong to this view as well as, for instance, the engravings on the dolmen at Gavrinis (page 20, right column) or Carschenna (page 20, left column).

In amplification of this view, and at the same time leading over to the developmental stages of the child in the first seven years, we come to the presentations of Rudolf Steiner (1911), in which he shows the stages of humanity in the course of the history of civilizations, passing from 'dream-like clairvoyant' vision to a conscious perception

Owens Valley (California)

of the surrounding world of the senses. Relics of the culture of old civilizations show us the relative position along this path of development. Are not children's drawings also impressions, 'footprints' on the path to human maturity?

We are familiar with the fact that during embryonic development the human being passes through stages that are physiologically similar

Pech-Merle (Lot)

18

Girl, 1 year 10 months

Carschenna (Graubünden)

Gavrinis (Brittany)

to animals. In the field of psychology, too, there are laws that reflect past phases of development. In the realm of childhood drawings we also find a repetition. At whatever age within the first seven years the child starts drawing it will begin at the two-year-old scribbling stage. If the child is already past that age, he will go through all the stages of creation in rapid succession, and stop at the motif corresponding to its development.

The understanding of the stages of civilization and the development of consciousness is increased when one sees them in connection with the periods of creation in children. In its drawings the child describes for us different conditions of consciousness, which are parallel with those of the cultural epochs. Time divisions within the first seven years show this phenomenon in a larger connection.

The earliest phase of children's drawings lasts to the third year. The next phase takes them to the threshold of five, and the third one from then till about the seventh year. Here are some examples to show these phases. First of all let us watch children at work.

In the first phase, *before the third year*, the process of creation arises in a dreamy way. Children are completely one with the rhythms that become visible on paper; they live entirely in the movement and are carried by it. Therefore, when asked by an adult, they are not is a position to explain the content.

The second phase, *after the third year*, is different. Now children let the arising picture take hold of their imagination. So whilst she draws Barbara says: 'Oh, that is a bear, and it has ears, more and more and bigger and bigger – and legs, lots and lots of them, and it runs with them...'

Andreas' attitude is typical of the third phase, *after the fifth year*. Whilst he is fetching his chalk and sitting up at the table he says, before he begins to draw...

'I am now going to draw Mr. Ackermann's house and dog ...' Andreas chooses a theme and the level of consciousness of his age permits a clear interpretation.

Let these aphoristically recorded glimpses suffice to indicate the first kind of classification that children's drawings teach us to see. In addition to this it would certainly be possible to make interesting investigations of the widest variety, but it would lead too far from the framework of this book. Now we will call on children themselves to help us understand their drawings. Our interest grows – associations appear – questions arise. Children possess their own vocabulary with which they convey their messages.

Boy, 1 year 11 months

Boy, 1 year 11 months

22

1. LINE AND MOVEMENT

Components of Pre-school Age Children's Drawings

'...[T]hat God in his firm decree chose the elements of straightness and of the curve to paint the divinity of the Creator into the world ... Thus the All-Wise devised the world of dimension whose whole being is contained in the differences of the straight and the curved line...'

Johannes Kepler, *De Harmonice Mundi*

Early Phase

'A circling, spiraling force and a force that moves up and down ...' (H. Strauss, 1932) show us the two paths of primeval movement in the symbolic language of children's drawings. The 'whirl of circles' and the 'archetypal cross' are formed out of these two creative principles. In the realm of drawn lines there are finally just these two possibilities: the straight and the curved line; the straight line that extends to infinity, and the curved line that continues until it makes a circle and can contract to a point. Kepler shows the cosmic-spherical origin of these two movements. In these rhythms he sees the divine handwriting, the primeval principle of creation.

The illustrations on page 22 enter straight into the living process of creation, a movement that reaches out and loops freely and then contracts into a knot; and in contrast to this there is a pendulum-swing in different directions.

In these drawings the child enters fully into the dynamic of the tendencies of movement described above; rotation and oscillation appear to have no beginning and no end. (Age barely two years.)

Gerhard Gollwitzer recommends for the drawing of a circular movement: 'Circle in the air like an eagle over the paper, until the circling gradually becomes visible in the drawn circle. You continue circling until at last – alas! you have to stop ...' The circling has been experienced to the full, and whoever has seen the joy children show when a knot or a 'ball' arises, can sense what it means to them.

The child does not rotate forever. The circling relaxes and the form now shows a movement that places the focal point in the middle. The child puts an accent there (adjacent). The movement that a moment ago was entirely taken up by the dynamic of rotation now becomes fixed, and after an energetic up-and-down it comes to rest. This shows the first suggestions of a path leading from outside inwards.

The drawing below makes it clear that the direction is getting more and more obvious; from out of the original field of the knot of whirls the flow of movement is increasingly acquiring an aim. The child slows the dynamic down. A balanced spiral movement becomes visible. One can still see the intensity of the circular movement in the living line of the curve. The movement appears to have come from far away and comes to rest on the paper. It curves in from far spaces with the aim of concentrating rapidly towards the middle. Again the accent is put in the place where the movement comes to a halt, where out of the circling on the periphery the inside is found. Up to the third year – unless there are exceptional circumstances – we only encounter spirals that move from outside inwards.

In the spirals in the above illustration the dynamic has come to rest; it has been directed into a balanced line of movement. Now it is no longer an eagle's flight nor a circling, which searches for and fixes an end; these curves are the tracks of a path that has been planned.

Whirl

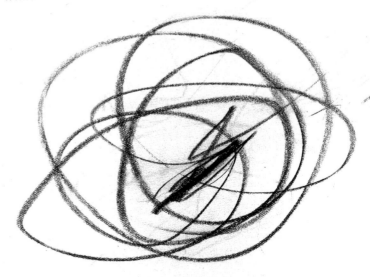

Girl, 1 year 10 months

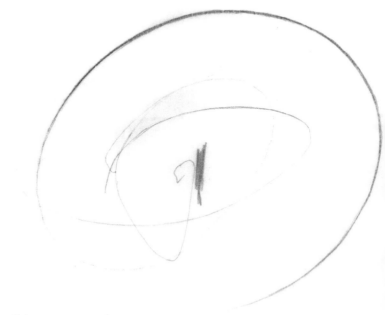

Girl, 2 years 2 months

Girl, 2 years 7 months

The fact that the line of movement, when it has reached the middle, does not turn round and swing from inside outwards again throws light on the situation of the child at this age.

About the third year children have reached a stage where it is possible for them to experience an inside and an outside. The first period of defiance marks the inner tension of this phase. By this time children have passed through three important stages of development. To begin with the attaining of the upright position brought about the first separation between the world and themselves. The gradual learning of language formed a new connection with other people. And lastly, at the conclusion of this first phase of development, the first beginnings of thought-formation crystallize (see K. König, *The First Three Years of the Child*).

In their drawings children now try very hard to make a circle and 'close it', 'join it up'. Every parent knows these efforts and will have experienced the intensity with which they tackle the task.

A little girl is sitting up at the table completely

Girl, 3 years 2 months

engrossed in drawing circles all over the page. It is her third birthday, and in answer to the question: 'What is your name?' the answer comes pat. 'I? My name is "I"!' This flash of ego-consciousness is documented in the child's drawing by the form of the circle.

Girl, 3 years 3 months

Girl, 2 years

Crossing

Before following the development of the circular form any further, we will link up with the first pendulum-like swinging movement. We will go back again in age to the second year. The same situation as with the circle is expressed in the realm of the straight line. The movement swings playfully back and forth on the page. To begin with it does not seem that a decision has been reached as to which direction to move in, but eventually two directions are prominent: the vertical and the horizontal.

The following illustrations (page 28 and 29) reflect the child's experience of standing upright. They illustrate from various aspects the attempt at mastering the perpendicular, the effort to acquire balance and the energy to maintain the upright position. Now the movement no longer swings vaguely in all directions but glides from above downwards and swings in loose whirls to the right. Horizontal lines with whirls at the end now join the perpendicular axis. These whirls hold the compositions in loose balance from above downwards and from right to left.

Are children repeating in picture form the streams of force that come into play when they struggle for the first time to raise themselves up? Let us remember how they had to pull themselves up by clutching on to the railings of their playpen, then later how they stood without holding on and practised keeping their balance. These efforts could hardly be drawn in a more living and pertinent way.

If in this drawing we can see children's first attempts to balance themselves, the following

Girl, 2 years 1 month

illustration shows us the tremendous energy required to maintain the upright position and to master it over and over again. The untiring practice, the child's hard work, is impressively mirrored here. Is not this line that rises up so resolutely into the perpendicular like a shout of triumph, an outburst of joy at learning to stand?

This resoluteness is behind all the further crosses, even when the dynamic of movement calms down to make way for abstract drawing.

The symbol of the cross documents standing in space. This orientation comes from a new impulse. In the drawing on the right column of page 29 we experience this impulse, this ego impact, in a most important way. Upright standing and walking distinguishes human beings and raises them above the animal kingdom.

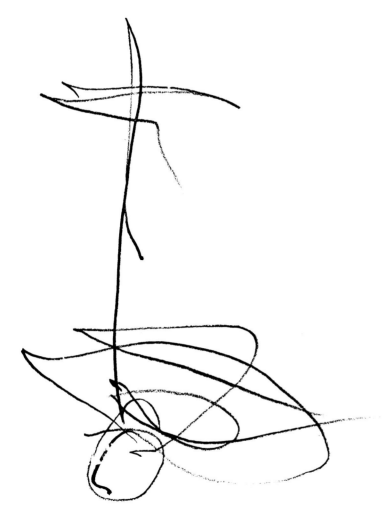

Boy, 1 year 9 months

David, just turned three, preferred a hard pencil, and let a mass of lines of the finest filigree arise on the paper, without, however, achieving the cross corresponding to his age. Then the family takes David and his younger brother to stay with friends who have five children. They are all older than David. David, the eldest up till now, the 'big' brother, cannot cope at the outset with his new role of 'little one'. So he escapes into illness, has a high temperature and lets himself be spoilt. Three days later he gets up and is well. As though to demonstrate that he can now master the new situation, he takes a thick coloured crayon and,

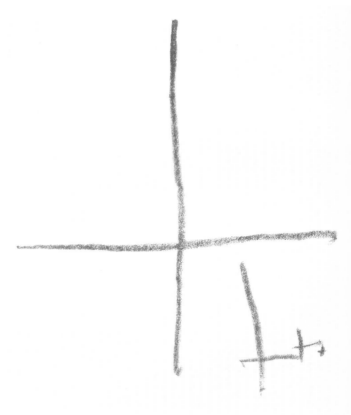

Boy, 2 years 7 months

29

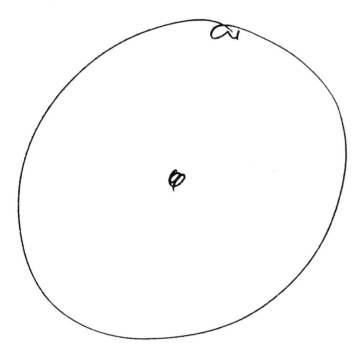

Girl, 3 years 3 months

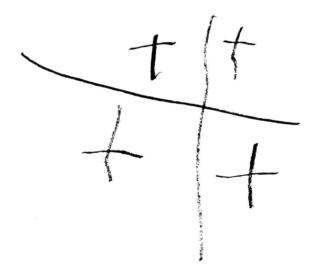

Boy, 3 years 6 months

for the first time, he draws, one after another, on several sheets of paper, a large perpendicular cross that fills a whole page.

We have followed the direction the drawings take, from the first knot of whirls to the form of the circle, and from the first weaving pendulum swings to the form of the cross. It is a path leading from the free rhythm of dynamic movement to the abstractness of geometry, from flowing creation to drawn forms. Before children carry out a further step and join together the symbols they have found in their language of forms, they put the point in their circle and extend the cross to become a star.

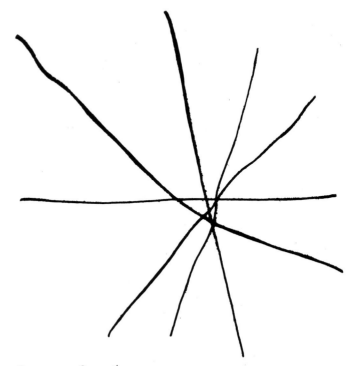

Boy, 3 years 6 months

Middle Phase

After the third year the circle and the crossing are fused into a unity, and they appear in the most diverse variations until the fifth year and beyond.

The circle, with its centre fixed by means of a point or a cross, describes the life situation of children at this age. They use these to show their relation to inner and outer space, and they put a point or a cross in the centre of the inner space to represent themselves. In both these symbols they illustrate for the first time their experience of the ego and of the world about them. The point and the cross within a circle represent the 'I-form'.

Whilst the children of today often call themselves 'I' very early, that is before the third year, we do not, even today, meet with the I-form in children's drawing before the third year. That would mean that this first important step towards finding themselves is not really accomplished until this time. Although children show the path leading to this formation before the third year, their handwriting is slack to begin with and is carried entirely by the dynamic of the movement. Not until abstract drawing appears do we see the conclusion of this process. Could this perhaps show the attentive observer the phenomenon of acceleration, the divergence between bodily and soul maturity in a new light? If so, it would be interesting to tell from any particular picture whether certain stages of development are still in the process of becoming or whether they have already reached a conclusion.

If we take another look at the origin of the point and the cross inside the circle, we shall be in-

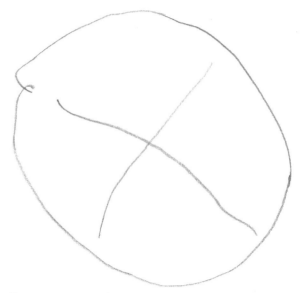

Boy, 3 years 7 months

terested – perhaps as parents – when looking at our children's drawings, to know whether they experience themselves in inner space as a point or as a cross. Their mode of expression throws light on their individual situation. We traced the transformation of the circling movement, and found that it starts as a sphere and contracts to a point. The rhythmic looping in harmony with the cosmos diminishes and a point now lies in the middle of the circle and starts creating a new arrangement around itself. The cross, the axial element, is placed in space. Here children experience the structuring of the environment through the forces emanating from themselves. If the first method is the expression of a more cosmic-soul element, then the second points to a more earthly-willing type.

In the same way as we can see the point (originally the whirl) and crossing as forms of soul

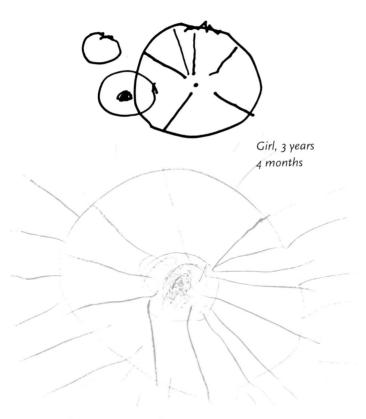

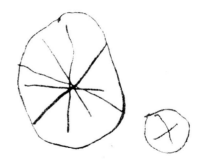

*Girl, 3 years
4 months*

Boy, 3 years 2 months

Girl, 3 years 9 months

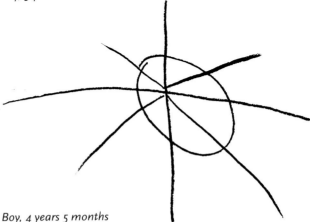

Boy, 4 years 5 months

experience, we can also find them in the middle and later phases of development indicating life-formative processes within the organism. Whirl and cross are also used here unconsciously as formulae. The whirl is used in drawing where the child senses living, flowing processes (see page 43). If we encounter the element of the crossing in the sphere of organs and functions, we can conclude that we are on the track of unconsciously perceived hardening processes. In the drawings on pages 44, 45, 56 and 58, they characterize the trunk. In the illustration on page 35 they represent the teeth-forming process (see Notes on the Study of Man).

Towards the fourth year a new orientation is on its way. The point and the crossing having crystallized as I-symbols, this concentration now gradually begins to loosen. The paths of movement lead from inside outwards. To begin with they radiate out from the centre as far as the periphery of the circle and remain within this boundary. This soon becomes more free, however, and groping feelers reach out beyond.

Late Phase

Towards the *fifth year* illustrative presentation pushes symbolic formulation more and more into the background. The composition of the child's vocabulary cannot, however, be concluded yet. Three essential principles of form, the circle, the square and the triangle, formally determine the main stages of children's creations. To start with, until the third year, the circle form is domi-nant; it is joined and partly replaced by the square and the rectangle. The triangle does not appear until about the fifth year and then it substantially influences the form.

Whilst surveying the element of children's early drawings, the collection of signs and symbols compiled by Rudolf Koch is worth noting. It includes astronomical and astrological symbols, the original signs of the alchemists which were used to associate substances with the four elements, and many others that have been used at

Scheme of child's vocabulary

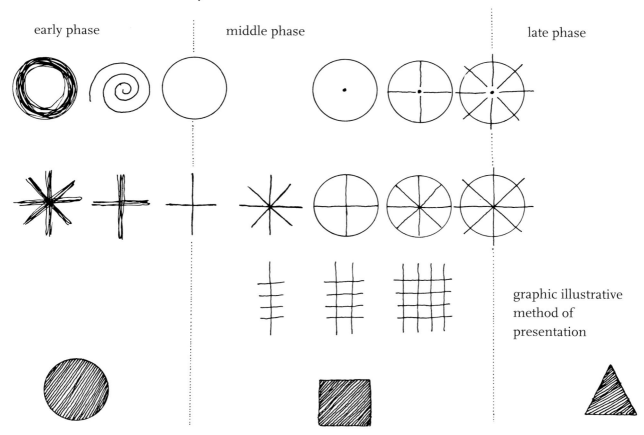

early phase   middle phase   late phase

graphic illustrative method of presentation

33

*Boy, 1 year
10 months*

different times to describe laws of evolution. If we leaf attentively through the small child's 'book of symbols' we will recognize many things that are familiar. Quite unconsciously the child lets us attend the birth of symbolic language.

The drawing on page 34 is only a 'scribble'. Rainer, who is not yet two years old, sits on the floor and has a piece of paper in front of him. He takes his crayons and a mass of lines arises on the page. He takes a blue, a red and then a black crayon, one after the other. He only casts a casual glance to see how the various lines come together to make a picture. What appears to interest him most whilst drawing is the activity. That is how this composition arises. It is a typical scribbled drawing, formed entirely out of the dynamic of this early phase, and so it can be put here to represent many a picture of this kind.

The intensity that is behind the crayon and that hurries to fill up the picture leads one to guess that it was dashed off in only a few minutes. Parents will hardly attach great importance to a scribble like this, and these early drawings usually wander into the waste-paper basket. Grown-ups judge them to be the first, unsuccessful attempts at drawing. It is rarely a piece of paper; more often it is the wallpaper, the floor, furniture or the pages of books that serve as the 'canvas' for these first scribbles.

Let us follow the build-up of such a page. The composition shows us three layers drawn one on top of the other: a blue, a red and a black one.

The underneath layer, that is the one drawn first in blue, shows a line of movement which is amazingly symbolic for this age; a loose circular movement out of which two streams of force flow.

In the red layer a pendulum-swing predominates. The blue movement released two streams of force, and now the next layer takes up this impulse again as a rhythm consisting of an up and down, rising and falling movement.

The third layer in black works from below towards the middle of the composition, and seems to be carried by a strong dynamic of the will.

In their movement tendency these three layers differ at some points strongly from one another. Polar opposites are there which bring about form in opposite ways. The first-drawn layer shows us a contrasting line of movement. The encircling blue keeps to itself, whilst the black movement is bursting with eruptive force. The red layer streams back and forth between these polar opposites.

In the further course of these descriptions it will become clear that all the elements of the human

Boy, 4 years 4 months

form already underlie an early scribble like this. These first compositions are still cryptic, still in a handwriting that is an experience of the process. The motif of the human being unconsciously motivates even the earliest scribbled drawings (age one year ten months).

The Picture of Man and the Picture of the Tree

'And he took the blind man by the hand, and led him out of the town; and when he had spit on his eyes, and put his hands upon him, he asked him if he saw aught. And he looked up, and said, I see men as trees, walking.'

St Mark 8.23-24

In the first seven years creative drawing is dominated by the motif of the human being. Children produce it in a new way at every stage and completely identify themselves with it.

The motif 'man' appears to spread out and include the motifs 'tree' and 'house' but these are not an extension of the choice of themes but only modifications of it. If we look back at historical records we find, for instance in the Edda, the original picture of the tree. The World Ash Yggdrasil grows out of primeval cosmic forces. The first time the human being is represented in children's drawings it bears the character of a tree, illustrating children's awareness of forces working in their own organism. The picture of the house includes the relationship to the world about them. In the course of the development of children the focus of their awareness of the forces working formatively within them shifts from one area to another. This produces different formulations of the same theme.

If one talks to children and asks them what they have drawn, as a rule one encounters a disarming openness when they explain their own 'work'. The information seems satisfactory until we discover that they give a totally different interpretation of the same picture to the next person who asks them. At one moment it is 'Granny' who has had her portrait drawn, the next moment it could be a 'car', a 'dog' or even a creation with an imaginary name: a 'goosety-boosety' or a 'kittenpillar'. When children take you by the hand and spirit you away to their world of fantasy you could believe that their pictures have a great number of motifs. But if you do not influence children when they are drawing they are usually not very interested in giving information, though there

Girl, 1 year 11 months

are exceptions to every rule. If children come to show you their pictures unasked, immediately after they have drawn them, and the urge to communicate finds its outlet in words, then the explanation is of great importance to them (see page 50). This also applies to many pictures that arise directly after waking up.

As in a seed there are a great number of possibilities in the above illustration. The basic elements of the curved and the straight line are germinally interwoven. Only gradually do the separate elements begin to emerge and the particular structures become recognizable. So figures arise that different children, unbeknown to each other, call 'a tree', 'a person' or 'a man' (see page 39). Tree and human being are a unity to begin with. In the child's presentation of a tree-man the 'ball' concentration is the 'roots'. The whole image grows and is formed out of this (see the blue layer on page 34). Streams of force move downwards and come together to form a 'trunk' (see the red layer on page 34). The tree-man at this early stage

Girl, 2 years

Boy, 2 years 1 month

39

is not connected to the earth. It hovers or rotates weightlessly in space. It is formed wholly out of the unconscious awareness of vegetative processes in which the children themselves are still immersed. So children are not at all surprised if the 'tree' has a human face or if the human form looks like the trunk of a tree.

Up till now the picture of the human being consists solely of 'head' and 'trunk'. When the limbs are added, a further characteristic process of differentiation begins. The movement that is dammed up at the lower end of the trunk, in a horizontal direction to the perpendicular, forms a firm basis at the bottom. This indicates 'finding their feet' for the first time.

The human being appears first of all as a pillar. Both feet are bound together as a unity, which

Girl, 2 years 3 months

Girl, 2 years 1 month

the figure stands on like a pedestal. This static position loosens up little by little and the figure begins to move. The arms are added horizontal to the body, and they are also joined together at the outer end.

About the third year, the first fixed sketch of the human form has been brought to a conclusion.

Girl, 2 years 6 months

Now it no longer hovers in space, rotating cosmically, but stands on the ground. Head, trunk and limbs are now incorporated into the figure in a symbolic way.

Beneath the surface a deep connection between the motifs of the tree and the human being persists beyond the first seven-year period. In later phases of life the drawing of a tree tells us a great deal about the individual qualities of a human being (compare Karl Koch, *The Tree-Test*).

The entry of the ego, that put the cross in the perpendicular, is what brings about the pillar-man. The forms in the drawings on pages 28 and 29 arise at the same time as this.

As the limbs are developed, the rigidity of the form softens. The hands and feet separate out more and more. During this phase the figures look almost like hovering marionettes. What was it like when the child was learning to walk? It fell over innumerable times after it had begun to move freely in space. But didn't it bounce up again immediately? Like a marionette suspended on a string the child regained the upright position at once.

Girl, 2 years 8 months

The Head

Beginning in the early phase of drawing and continuing on into the late one, children represent the head as a round form closed in itself. They add eyes, mouth and nose as essential characteristics of the human physiognomy. The children have now found their formula for drawing a face, and they carry on applying it symbolically without changing it much. Even up to the fifth year they keep to the front view of the face. The profile does not come until later on.

The Trunk

Cecilia (three years six months) is busily drawing. And whilst her crayon glides across the paper, she says: ... that is a tree-trunk, and it is turning into a man'. This is a new approach. Up till now the crayon circled round the spherical form of the head, and the rest of the body was added to this. Now, after the third year, the focal point of the picture is in the trunk part. The human form arises out of the tree 'trunk'.

All the pictures have in common this orientation round an axis of symmetry. This determines the vertical direction and forms that backbone of the figure. The impulse to stand upright gave it the vertical orientation. This experience of uprightness now determines the form. The trunk, in both senses, is pulled out lengthwise. Rhythmic pendulum-swings and whirls, a rhythmic

Girl, 3 years 3 months

43

Girl, 3 years 4 months

Boy, 3 years 10 months

flow and rhythmic repetition all play their part in the form of this 'trunk' of the human form. Children present three different picture elements and realms of experience in their drawing of the trunk.

The drawing on page 43 arises when the child inwardly observes the fluid process. A metamorphosis takes place. The original pendulum stream of the 'trunk' now whirls round the axis. The circulation of fluids, the flow of the spinal fluid that gently pulsates with the breathing, appears to determine the form here.

Another aspect: This time the axis is not surrounded by flowing movements, but branch-like structures lead off from it to right and left. In this phase of children's drawing the picture of the tree finally separates out from the picture of the human being. The tree's branches reach out into space and are provided with leaves on the ends.

We notice a totally different development in the following drawings. Here lines are crossing the axis of symmetry. The upright orientation needs static struts. The original flowing element hardens and forms scaffolding resembling a skeleton.

In this way the 'ladder' arises. It is marked out rhythmically with sub-divisions. The spinal column is divided up and the ribs encompass the chest. The rib cage has arisen in picture-form. Every parent knows the ladder motif, which appears in all drawing books and is often the child's chief mode of expression for quite a long time. We will meet with the ladder again in house pictures.

Girl, 3 years 6 months

Boy, 3 years 7 months

Boy, 4 years 5 months

45

The Limbs

The trunk, which the children have for some time been concentrating their attention on, now has arms and legs added. In contrast to the static rigidity of the lower limbs the arms are, from the very beginning, more mobile. In the middle phase the children hurry to draw these in character before doing so with the legs and feet. The 'arms' grow disproportionally long and make contact with the world about them. They are formed like organs of perception, and their sphere extends a long way beyond the child's own body. The hands, either flashing out rays or ending in whirls, still clearly show this great liveliness.

Girl, 3 years 4 months

Girl, 3 years 6 months

Girl, 4 years 4 months

The presentation of feet takes the longest time. In complete contrast to the limb-like feelers of arms and hands their formation starts with a concentration and thickening. A thrust of forces which are of a completely uncontrolled will-nature are built into the form with the power of an eruption. This appears to come from outside the human form. This impulse is often so strong that there is hardly room on the page any more for the drawing of the head and the trunk (see drawing above). This intensity of will is the same force that was expressed in the black layer of the early scribble drawing (page 34) or as the legs of the horse show us (page 70). The blocks that human beings walk on or the stumpy, pillar-like foundation of the figure on the following page, also arise out of these thrusting forces.

In earliest childhood, whilst still in the cradle, children 'discover' their hands. Their hands are amongst their first playthings. Towards the fourth year they begin to draw hands. But it seems to be obvious from the pictures that they have no idea how many fingers a hand has. Only sometimes chance has it that the number is correct. Besides, it doesn't seem to matter to children whether it is 'right', as they are not yet interested at this stage of development in a naturalistic likeness. On the contrary, they note them down in the way they experience them. The inner life process and not the external form is the determining factor. So the boy who places his human figure on power-ful foundations is not at all robust but a slender delicately built child (page 48).

As we saw, the first rough draft of the human form is brought to a conclusion by about the third year. The figure manifests out of a cosmic-embryonic, hovering condition. The pillar-man arises. He stands on the earth. The working out

47

of the form, the differentiation of the limbs, follows. This adds the direction of movement to the right and left to the spatial orientation of upwards and downwards. The presentation of the human being describes a process that takes place from above downwards. The forming process begins with the head. The differentiation and structuring of the trunk follows, and the arms and legs are attached last of all. We see the same order being followed in the development of children's bodies up until the first organic change; from babyhood to the change of teeth they have, step by step, taken possession of their body (see Notes on the Study of Man).

At the time when the 'tree-man' occurs, children are in a phase of their development that remains shut to their memory. Not until the time when they are developing their limbs do they have memory pictures. The child's consciousness now comes forth from out of a 'dream-condition' and in the course of its development it turns actively towards the world outside. The development of the human image in children's drawings bears witness to these stages. A path is described to us, which passes from an unconscious sleeping awareness of formative forces to a waking grasp and initial reproducing of human beings and the world around them.

Does St Mark the Evangelist portray a similar process in his description of the healing of the blind man? Does not the blind man pass through similar stages whilst he is acquiring his eyesight? Does not this description show us a related experience to the one that children's drawings show us, namely a process of consciousness taking place in rapid succession?

◁ *Boy, 5 years 6 months*

Boy, 2 years 7 months
'Child in Heaven'

50

The Human Being and the House

The house that enfolds us

'Child in Heaven' is what Rainer calls the drawing (page 50). The 'child', a little tree-man, is already familiar to us, and he is surrounded by a circular movement, which is 'heaven'.

The picture below, too, describes a cosmic situation.

This time it is not a tree-man that is in the centre. Do not these 'small people' with head and limbs remind one of the embryonic state? These pictures confirm Grözinger's assumption that even in the archetypal knot of whirls an unconscious memory of the embryonic state is being expressed: 'A being ... that was in his mother's body two years ago, washed by moisture, like the fish in the sea...' It is a kind of 'memory' of this prenatal state, but even more than this; it is an awareness of forces that enclose and shape it. Rudolf Steiner describes how, in our development after physical birth, we human beings go through further 'births': 'Just as we are enclosed within the physical sheath of our mother up to the time of our birth, we are enclosed in an etheric sheath up till the change of teeth, that is, till about the seventh year.' In these drawings not only the embryonic state of the body appears in picture form but also the perception of this 'etheric sheath' (see Notes on the Study of Man).

The archetypal knot of whirls is already a 'house' and is depicted by children as a sheath, as the state of being enclosed. So we can understand that many children return again and again to drawing the ball of whirls, even at an age when they have long outgrown this early phase of drawing. Does not perhaps our habit as an adult of rolling up into a 'sphere' before going to sleep belong here? By bending our knees and drawing them up close to our body we approach the embryonic position. We seek sleep within the safety of the sphere.

Girl, 3 years

A house to shut oneself up in shows a different relationship to the world. A new form of house demonstrates the increasing independence of the soul of the child. The children experience the close unity between themselves and the world growing weaker and weaker. The spherical, cosmic house is replaced by a form that stands at the bottom of the page. The space inside begins to fill the whole page. We see the family – father, mother, brothers and sisters – living in the house.

In the illustration on page 53 we not only find father and mother at home, but two circles have moved in too. We know all the people living in this house. We have not only followed the course of the origin of the tree-man, but also of the circle with a centre point. (See Chapter 1) Is this house occupied by four people, or are the people being illustrated from two different aspects – on the one hand the physical and on the other the soul-spiritual? Whatever it is, the combination of an abstractly drawn presentation with figure illustration points to several realms working simultaneously in the child's unconscious experience.

In their shape these houses still keep a part of their spherical roundness, which is based on the construction of the 'bee-hive', the classical archetypal house. Nevertheless a new process is starting in that the children are beginning to sense and perceive the distance between themselves and the surrounding world. This results in a house-form arising in which the square or rectangle predominates. This house is like a box where the walls fit snugly round the figures and there can be a really tight fit. The children move out of their cosmi-

Boy, 3 years 7 months

cally rounded dwelling into their earthly house of the cube (page 54). The narrowing down in the perception of cosmic realms through the acquiring of selfhood – the process of becoming an 'I' – resembles an encapsulating of the soul. The house-form arising from this is based on the right angle.

Let us look at the games of four-year-olds. All parents know how much their children love building a house out of chairs, tables and sheets, to creep into. It is a game where one builds up around one the world one experiences.

The close connection of the first three years with the world that we adults cannot see, grows weaker. The new relationship to the world causes

Girl, 4 years 1 month

Girl, 4 years 1 month

questions to arise that can sometimes put parents in a moral dilemma. The old 'state of Paradise', the conviction of the Almightiness of God, is now questioned. Reiner's statement about 'the gate that is shut and nobody may go in any more – and people who doubt, and the sun shines ...' belongs to this phase, and so does David's sad story: 'When God awoke He was sad because He was too weak to kill the devil. So an angel helped Him and killed the devil for Him – that is why God was sad, because He was too weak ...' Or the problem: 'Mummy, does it ever happen that God the Father creates an angel and it won't do because it isn't beautiful enough. So what does he do with it? Does He send it away, or what does He do with it?'

To the same extent that children notice the world around them more clearly they also begin to register the difference between themselves and other people. Their questions become

Girl, 4 years 2 months

realistic: 'Mummy, how big are the babies when God puts them into their mother's tummy?' Or: 'Mummy, when the mother eats milk pudding, does the baby in her tummy have a taste too?'

The change in their life interest also determines the kind of drawings children do. An interest in function awakens. The house acquires a door now – with a handle, of course. This is the 'door opener and shutter' and it is never forgotten. Otherwise how could one open the door to get out and in? Before this the children lived with their whole being completely in the activity. The child and the action were one. Now they come to the stage of perceiving activities in their surroundings. So George (age four years six months) characterizes the members of the family like this: 'The Daddy, he is the busy-man, and the Grandpa, he is the cigar-man, and the Granny, she is the watching one.'

Boy, 4 years 7 months

Girl, 4 years 6 months

In house pictures windows appear now as well as doors. The view extends towards the outside. Inside, the furnishing of the house begins; the chimney-pot smokes, it is nice and warm and the figure on the bed relaxes comfortably (page 55). The newly acquired setting is given embellishments. We are drawn into the room, we see windows, shutters and curtains and even perhaps a picture on the wall.

But children do not stop here, when they have reached the aspect of the house described above. The walls are opened up; one is now not only in the house but at the same time one also faces the house. The outside of the house appears. Door

and windows and – quite new – someone is looking out of the window (above left).

The children have now left two stages behind: They were shut in the house, and they made it into a comfortable home. Without renouncing these two stages they now take a third step; they acquire the ability to look from outside at the house and the people looking out of it. Questions like the following arise out of this new situation. Nelly, the little girl from Berlin, asks: 'Mummy, how did God make eyes? I want to know exactly how He managed to make the eyes turn round in the head – do you see, like this ... I want to know exactly how He made hair, to get it to grow out of

56

the head, like this – do you see, like this ... And the sun, tell me Mummy, how did He make the sun?' Mother: 'He made a big shining ball and put it in the sky.' 'No, Mummy, the sun is the sun and not a ball – that would have fallen down again ...'

In addition to the ever-increasing amount of thought content in the drawing we meet with yet another way of drawing houses. We encountered the ladder motif at the stage when the human form was acquiring the upright posture. It occurs when a flowing element begins to harden (page 45). The vertical crossed by the horizontal demonstrates standing in space. The ladder is based on the static element of the crossing as the basis of construction. If this element continues to harden, the lattice occurs. The 'tower' arises out of the symbol of the ladder and the lattice. In the tower motif the skeleton becomes a house.

Skeleton as House

The human form is as though locked up in this static state, and becomes architecture itself. Even the head is completely incorporated in this principle, and the eyes do not gaze freely into the world but have become slits in the tower (page 56, on the right). Are we not reminded of popular fairy tale motifs? Is not Rapunzel, for instance, locked up in a tower like this, waiting for the prince who can release her from the prison?

The phenomenon of fear stands in direct connection with the shutting in of the individuality. Little children do not mind being left alone at night – but then, when they grow 'older and more sensible' they scream at night and call for their mother. They beg their parents to leave the door open in the evening and the light on outside. Fear has its origin within the human being. The dog in the street or any other threat from outside does not primarily produce it. Fear occurs when the unquestioned oneness with the world is lost, when children have moved step by step into the abode of their body and this becomes denser and denser. The tower and the lattice illustrate these steps. The process is like breathing in. We are in danger of suffocating, of getting cramp, if we do not have the chance to breathe out again.

Klaus' drawing (page 58, on the left) gives us a striking illustration of this situation. It finds its complement in the pendulum-beat in the opposite direction. Peter (on the right) also bases his drawing on the statics of the ladder but round its rungs life begins to stir. Semi-circular curves unfold like the annual rings of a tree. Then it grows and grows in rhythmic repetition. Enter-

Boy, 5 years 2 months   *Boy, 5 years 6 months* ▸

ing again into life processes the structure could extend forever.

Rhythm determines this stage of development. What was closed can now open, what had hardened can become soft. Breathing, looping forms enliven and expand what was rigid and they entwine around the static base. In play too, hiding away in the house they have built themselves or soaring blissfully on the swing or the seesaw – at this stage children enjoy extremes to the full (see Notes on the Study of Man).

In no other motif can one see the multiple experiences in the process of human incarnation so clearly as in the motif of the house. On the one hand the process of moving into the house leads to becoming shut off. One is now completely dependent on oneself. On the other hand, when one

has taken possession of the house, the door to the world opens from inside. By means of these drawings the children show us a path that leads through heights and depths, joy and sorrow, good fortune and bad.

58

Head-and-Feet People – Head-and-Limb People

Another shape of the human form is added after the fourth year to the great variety of children's forms of expression. The child finds a completely new approach to the picture of man. The 'head-and-feet person' or 'head-and-limb person' arises. These pictures are very popular with grown-ups. With their humorous, easily remembered appearance they represent for many people the symbolic language of early childhood. They appear relatively late in the course of the child's development. Children like drawing them by the dozen and they fill whole pages of drawing books.

We ask ourselves: Why do children at this age look for a new form of the human being in their drawings? Haven't they already just found a convincing presentation of the human form, the tree-person? Where is the key to an understanding of this phenomenon? Are children showing

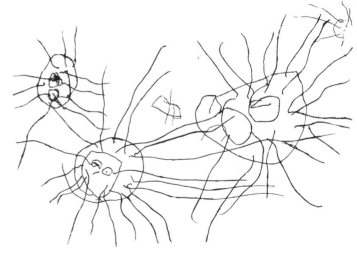

Girl, 4 years

us a new realm of their experience in presenting the human being as a head-and-feet person and a head-and-limb person? The vocabulary of form symbols comes to our aid. The circle arose as the first form complete in itself. Its creation dominates the early phase of drawing. By the third year it has become a symbol. This concludes the development of a form. The circle becomes a formula for 'head' (sometimes with the addition of a face), a symbol of the 'I', and

Boy, 4 years

Boy, 3 years 9 months

59

Girl, 4 years 4 months

determines the earliest form of the 'house'.

Not until after children have demonstrated, in the circle containing a middle point, their first step to egohood, and are then in the next stage seeking contact with the world outside, do the drawings of the head-and-feet and head-and-limb people appear. The human form becomes all 'head', completely spherical. Every sun with its rays – whether it has a face or not – is the illustrative version of the abstract symbol of a circle with structures leading out from the centre.

It is of help to us to know that Lersch (quoted by Grözinger) has ascertained that the human being in an early stage of development can be compared with a round sensitive sphere 'upon the periphery of which the influences of the world make an impact ...'. There is something in children that responds to these influences and they extend their limb-like 'feelers' towards them.

The head-and-feet and head-and-limb people mirror the development and the activity of the senses in an especially impressive way. We could well imagine that these antennae convey the subtlest perceptions.

The tree-man of the early stage had already ac-

Boy, 4 years 2 months

Girl, 5 years

quired 'feet' too (pages 40 and 41). They were added on when the form attained the upright position. These first feet arise out of an inner feeling for this newly acquired position. The head-and-feet people are distinguished from the head-and-limb people by apparently being more aware of that which is connected with their own body. The 'limbs' raying out from the head-and-limb person belong to a realm of the senses that registers perceptions outside the body. The 'fringes of feeling' must be thought of chiefly as organs of taste and sight, getting to know the world by sniffing about and spying around.

Solar plexus

In another place we find similar elements of construction to those upon which the drawings of the head-and-feet people and the head-and-limb people are based.

In the presentation of head-and-feet people and head-and-limb people the structures feel their way beyond the periphery of the circle. In the drawings at the top of page 32 the periphery forms the boundary. The lines of force remain within the circle. A 'sun-wheel', a 'steering-wheel'

61

arises. The human form has a symbol like this in the area of the navel. David interprets these forms by saying: 'Mummy, everybody has their own steering wheel there (describing a circle round the area of his navel). My steering-wheel is bigger than yours, and if it gets bigger and bigger and doesn't fit inside any longer, then people die.' We must look on this symbol as the sign of the solar plexus, an essential part of the vegetative nervous system (see Notes on the Study of Man).

Girl, 5 years

2. FROM LINE TO SURFACE

Colour as the Medium of Soul Expression

'Colour is the soul of nature and of the whole cosmos, and we share in this soul when we experience colour.'

Rudolf Steiner

Colour, as a new means of expression, is added to the drawing of lines in the middle phase of the development of drawing. The line ceases to be an adequate expression by itself. With the world of colour a new realm of experience opens.

Barbara (three years nine months) gives us an example of the transition from drawing with lines to the drawing of a coloured surface (page 64). Let us try and see how she has gone about it. A strongly dynamic movement makes a bizarre shape. Suddenly this seems to be lifted up to another dimension – it begins to fan out on the surface.

David (three years eight months) has dipped his brush in the colour and calls out: 'Mummy, look, I have just been singing with the brush.' Cecilia (four years one month) carefully chooses some crayons from her box of colours, and whilst she is drawing she says: 'A lot of yellow and pink must be in it so that it will be really happy because Daddy is coming.' Or on another occasion: 'Do everything dark, Mummy is still in hospital.'

Three childish remarks about the same activity. David's happy shout is an immediate expression of the soaring flight, the 'melody' of the movement that his brush has just carried out. A composition of rhythmic lines arises on his paper. With Cecilia it is different. In her pictures the colours yellow and pink, or the darkness, begin to spread out as a surface. If David's picture shows us the rhythm of movement, then Cecilia's composition is based on the feeling of joyful anticipation – because her father is coming – or of someone sadly missing – her mother is still in hospital. She chooses the colour which accords with her feelings. So it becomes a medium of soul expression. The joy of creation inspiring David and Cecilia arise from different sources, out of the rhythm of movement and out of the soul.

Before their third year children use colour to emphasize the line. The joys in endless repetition made them keep on choosing different colours. When the dark one took over from the light one, the child was primarily interested in the process of consolidating the lines of movement (early phase). Towards the fourth year, which is in the middle period, a new element appears. Touched by the nature of colour the soul of the child becomes creative. When the world of feeling comes into drawing, the world of colour comes into it too.

Children's illnesses can play a decisive role; they often open the way to the realm of colour. The pictures tend to consist more and more exclusively of surfaces of colour. The circles, bor-

Girl, 3 years 9 months

ders, ladders, rectangles and squares are filled up like a chequered cloth (page 65).

Already from an early age children react to particular colours with sympathy or antipathy. They prefer or reject certain colours. Before children use colour for drawing objects, we meet it as an elemental force, a medium with which they create freely. They choose a colour according to its soul quality and in this way they find their own colour symbolism. So they unconsciously put warm tones beside cold ones, happy ones opposite sad ones, aggressive ones opposite passive ones. Any material that comes to hand is welcome. Their need for self-expression is so great that they are even capable of drawing varying colour surfaces with an unsuitable crayon. The compositions (for instance, on pages 62, 67 and 69) are colour creations that resound. They are made up of particular intervals in the tone range. The climax of this kind of creation is reached towards the fifth year. Then children try out the whole register of colour tones. A riot of colour arises. The individual colours meet each other and overlap. New colour combinations arise on the paper to which they react sensitively. A living dialogue develops. The more subtly it is experienced the more varied the colour range becomes. If we were to encounter some of these pictures in an art exhibition of modern paintings we would be eager to find the name of the artist in the catalogue.

The descriptions of Jacques Lusseyran, who went blind in his seventh year, form a bridge to the experience of colour. What he was able to keep alive right into his adult years in the way of inner experience of light and colour can show us the impulse with which the child approaches colour: '... the moment I lost the light of my eyes,

I found the light undiminished in myself. I did not have to remember what this light had been for my eyes to keep the memory of it alive. The light was there, in my spirit and in my body. It was imprinted on them in its entirety. The light was there, accompanied by all the visible forms, colours and lines, possessed of the same strength that it has in the world of the eyes.

'I repeat: the experience vouchsafed to me was not memory. The light I continued to see without my eyes was the same as before. But my standpoint in relation to the light had changed. I had moved closer to its origin ... when I was sad, when I was afraid, all shades became dark and all forms indistinct. Then I was joyous and attentive, all pictures became light. Anger, remorse, plunged

Boy, 4 years 3 months

everything into darkness; a magnanimous resolution, a courageous decision radiated a beam of light. By and by I learnt to understand that love meant seeing and that hate was blindness, was night ...'

Jacques Lusseyran shows us that colour is a mediator of soul experience but Andreas (five), too, expresses his connection with it extraordinarily clearly when he calls out to his mother: 'Sing a cheerful song, that is such a lovely red', or: 'White is such a stiff colour – sort of stiff – a sting is white like that' ... 'It hurt very much, a yellow hurt with black spikes.' How directly soul quality becomes colour experience!

The statement that monkeys belong to the ranks of gifted painters may be shocking, perhaps. By

Girl, 4 years 5 months

experimenting with chimpanzees and gorillas, Morris shows us that these animals paint with delight and have a highly developed feeling for colour. Monkeys certainly do not achieve a conscious form though they can lay on colour in various ways. They lack that which works in the child, namely a formative force that rises in self-awareness above the surgings of the soul. Monkeys are also gifted in the graphic arts. Their dynamic curves compete well with those of children. Several pages drawn by 'monkey hand' have fetched high prices at auctions in recent years. Why shouldn't the element of movement in which they live so strongly, all the swinging and leaping they do, enable these highly developed animals to draw in a living, dynamic way? Of course, at the point where the shaping of

67

movement sets in with children and the decisive impulses manifest themselves in their drawings, animals are incapable of carrying out this step. Neither can monkeys achieve the I-forms of the crossing and the circle.

Boy, 5 years

Boy, 6 years 5 months

3. FROM SYMBOL TO ILLUSTRATION

Graphic-illustrative Compositions

Children's first drawings follow a cosmic movement that knows neither outside nor inside. They mirror a situation in which they themselves are. About the third year, the first step towards independence is expressed in the way children intentionally draw circles and straight lines. They are unconsciously aware of the formative processes working in their organism. These become formulae for drawing. Soul processes find their expression in the realm of colour. Towards the end of the fifth year, with their newly acquired distance, the children's gaze turns to the objects in their surroundings. They take shape and are firmly placed on the ground. Everyday matters are observed and reproduced. The world of their own life-processes and functions steps into the background of their awareness. Their perception turns in another direction. Their gaze turns outwards.

Imagination is woven into the child's drawing. This reveals the close connection between the forces of memory and the child's own experiences. Imagination is born after the third year and from now on it adorns everything. Up till now we encountered this soul experience in the realm of colour or it was established as a formula (illustrations of circle, cross and lattice). Soul experience now becomes pictorial presentation.

Children's souls 'play' with what they have experienced and what they remember, and it is lifted up into their imagination. A narrative-illustrative element arises.

We meet different levels of experience; wide-awake observations and dreamy awareness, things seen and things felt are often all mixed up in the same picture. The drawings illustrate transitions and overlapping of the most varied realms of perception.

Tommy's and Reiner's drawings show all these levels of experience, the swing from one level of consciousness to another. A horizontal line divides Tommy's picture (page 72, on the left) into an upper and a lower realm. This is like a dividing line of consciousness. A house stands in the upper part of the composition with a door, windows, and roof – in fact everything that is essential to a house is put in. A house is represented in the lower half, too, but this arises directly out of the 'ladder and lattice motif'. Two presentations of the same theme in one and the same picture; in the top half the front of the house is drawn from memory, in the lower half the child's experience of his own soul and bodily nature is reflected. Let us remember the 'ladder and lattice motif'; it expressed being shut in, beginning to become separate. This feeling is joined by clear observation and the faculty of memory. The house as a memory-picture arises.

Reiner draws his birthday table (page 72, on the right). It is decorated with candles and stands in

Boy, 5 years

Boy, 4 years 7 months

front of wallpaper with birds and stripes printed on it. But to our surprise, in the middle of the room, beside the birthday table, the ancient mythical symbol of the 'tree-man' has been put in. So an old formula is being retained here too, and symbolically incorporated in the description of a memory of the outside world.

A new language of gesture is applied in drawing. The emphasis is laid on what appears to be of importance to the child. Claudia describes the full drama of a pictorially told action. The soul gesture has here become bodily (from a story: '... and she stretched out her hand wide ...'; illustration on page 73, on the left).

In the illustration of 'Granny giving the baby its bottle', the size of the two figures shows their relative importance in the eyes of the child. 'Granny' is small and insignificant, the 'baby' gigantic in comparison (illustration on page 73, on the right).

Eugen's drawing elucidates the newly acquired distance from things (page 74). A line divides the page into two parts. A dividing line is drawn between the sphere of heaven where the sun, the moon and the stars are, and the earth on which human beings stand. This division between the sky and the earth will be found in all the following drawings.

Girl, 4 years 10 months

Girl, 4 years 9 months

Before the fifth year the children are hardly in a position to organize and arrange the elements of the picture. To begin with they register the multitude of perceptions and put them all down on the paper in a summary way. For example, Ingrid (four) makes a résumé of her holiday in Switzerland by drawing all mixed up in one picture: the family of father, mother, brothers and sisters; the sun, the animals and the mountains.

All the objects drawn so far were quite naturally subjected to the two-dimensional quality of the paper. Just as for thousands of years humanity used a non-spatial method of presenting objects, children express themselves in drawing by projecting on to a flat surface. Now, towards the fifth year, the problem of three dimensions arises. Children start experimenting. The profile is added to the front of the face.

Grotesque 'howlers' occur when newly acquired elements of observation are mixed up with old symbolic forms. Thus a human face presented in profile can, for instance, have two eyes side by side like a flounder, an abnormally large mouth which, as a left-over from the front view, goes a long way across the cheek, and perhaps two ears as well, one on each side of the head (see Hans Meyers, *Die Welt der kindlichen Bildnerei* and

Boy, 5 years 6 months

Gustav Britsch, *Theorie der bildenden Kunst* [*The world of children's modelling* and Gustav Britsch, *Theory of plastic art*]). So long as children were in the position of presenting things solely according to the way they experience them, nothing like this could happen. Now that they have begun to incorporate objects from the surrounding world in their drawings these strange combinations occur. In the realm of colour they try out what can be produced by mixing colours ... 'What does red and mauve make ... brown and blue ... brown and green? Ah, a beetle ...' (Cecilia). Colour becomes form.

Not until observations are made from a distance can the presentation break loose from the immediate drama of the witnessed event and allow for new criteria in the arrangement of things. Now children become more and more capable of basing their drawings on thought-out pictures. A new element is added to the array of separate

Girl, 4 years 5 months

75

Girl, 5 years 10 months

objects. Now for the first time one can speak of an artistic arrangement of the page. The child's observations become systematic, freely usable, repeatable thought pictures. The step is taken from the kind of memory that is confined to a definite situation to that of a freely usable memory picture. A new realm of thought opens up.

Henceforth all the pictures of the human beings are based on naturalistic ideas. So the difference between men and women is now illustrated. The children are carefully dressed and walk or dance with shoes on their feet. Hair bows, apron strings and striped socks are drawn down to the last detail. The particular event is minutely described; the mishap of the little girl who has fallen over, whilst her friends dance gaily to the tunes on their instruments.

At long last animal forms are also included in the child's drawings, though to begin with from the human point of view. The early formation of the human form, the combination of head and 'trunk' is tipped over from the vertical into the horizontal and supplied with an endless number of 'feet'. It takes some time before these 'centipedes' turn into animals one can ride on. They gradually individualize out of a fixed formula (page 77).

After the fifth year horses begin to play a prominent part. It seems to fascinate children and they feel the urge to draw horses even when there are none in their immediate town surroundings. A 'Mexican in a Mexican hat' is riding on David's horse (page 70). Could the physiognomy of a horse's face possibly be drawn more character-

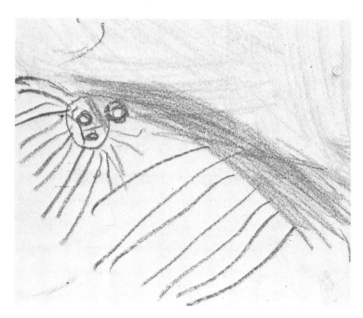

Girl, 3 years 8 months

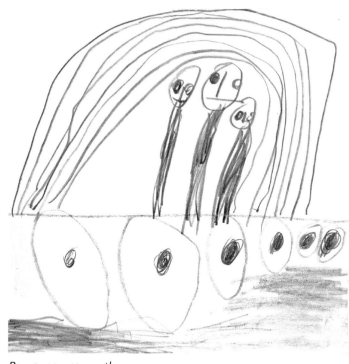

Boy, 3 years 11 months

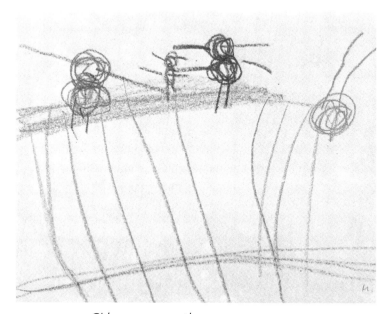

Girl, 4 years 5 months

Boy, 4 years 8 months

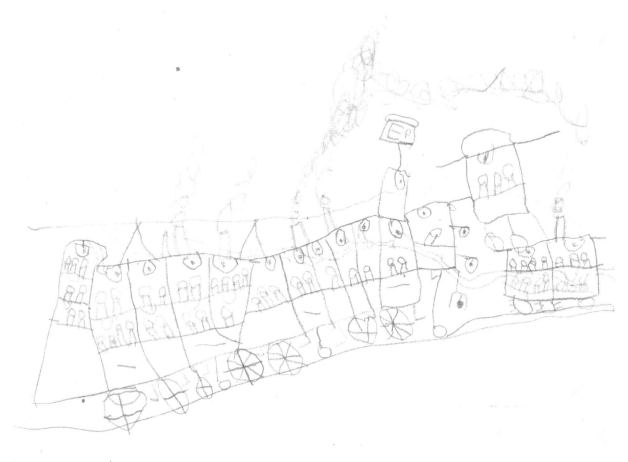

Boy, 4 years 9 months

istically: the teeth, the inflated nostrils, the intelligent eyes and the alertness in the cocked ears? The horse's legs are stocky and remind one of the people's feet and legs on pages 47 and 48. With this animal, too, the limbs still arise out of the child's own experience, that is, out of the thrust of the forces that made such an impression on us in the black layer of the early scribble-stage drawing (page 34).

Now one could ask: what about the presentation of mechanical objects like cars, aeroplanes, trains, etc.? It is a mistake to think that the fascination of technology and the interest in our modern means of transport induces the child to make pictures of them. By closer observation we will see that the cars, ships, trains or aeroplanes are only an extension of the house illustration. To start with, houses on wheels, houses on the waves or lots of houses coupled together on wheels represent our present-day mechanical means of locomotion.

Girl, 6 Years
'Zoo'

79

Girl, 6 years

Boy, 6 years 7 months

81

Girl, 6 years

Colour is added to the illustrative form of presentation. The compositions now have a strongly formalistic character and they can thrill us with their bold construction. The triangle occurs more and more often. The happy child in the above picture, or the tent-shaped house in which one is protected beneath the starry heavens (page 80), are entirely subject to the law of the obtuse angle. A three-cornered gable is placed on top of the rectangle of the previous phase (page 81).

Martin's picture (page 83) shall be put here to represent the style of the six-year-old. Martin does not go to school yet but he has formed his idea of a schoolroom from his big brother's accounts. So he makes a picture for us of how school appears to him. At the top left, he is on the way to school; now he has arrived at the schoolhouse, which has fir trees growing round it. A clock – time already plays a part! – though it is just a pretend one with mirror-image figures. Rows of attentive pupils are sitting behind desks. Each one has a slate and a duster in front of them. The teacher is explaining something at the blackboard. She has a crown on; a royal head covering distinguishes her. Two companions have crept into the classroom with him; he either met them on the way to school or brought them with him from his play-corner at home. One of them is sitting with cocked ears between the children in the back row; the other has settled down under the blackboard.

Just as Martin does us an extraordinarily precise drawing of his conception of the schoolroom, Matthias (six) describes his experience in words. Seeing a man in brightly coloured uniform has intrigued him. That evening he realizes: 'I can still see the man when I want to; then I put him in front of my eyes ...' (Quoted in Hattermann, *Werdestufen der frühen Kindheit* [Stages of early childhood]). Could a free memory-picture possibly be more exactly defined?

The result of the school-age child's new state of consciousness is that the spontaneous creative-artistic impulse begins to wane. It belongs to the unhappy experience of those people interested in the drawings of children to witness that their expressiveness now grows weaker and weaker. On entering the second seven-year period the ability to reproduce as such what they sense in their own life forces disappears. The first organic change as well as the change of teeth makes it clear to us that the processes that have been building up

Boy, 5 years 10 months

and refining the child's organism so far, are now becoming free for other tasks (see Notes on the Study of Man).

The forces that motivated the drawings showed us steps in the process of 'coming into the body', 'moving into the house'. As a seismographic record the 'house' man appears before us. The first things we see are the rough plans of the scribble stage, which flow entirely out of the dynamic of movement. By the third year the first structure of the 'rough brick-work' has been set up and is made manifest in the 'pillar-man' as well as in the circle and the cross. Finally comes the refining and developing; this is concluded with the first organic change.

The first plans for the building of this house appeared to be drawn up by forces apparently outside the child's body, forces that left their traces on the drawing paper through the medium of the child. We see processes guiding the crayon, which arise from different realms of activity; form, rhythm and will all leave their mark. In the various phases, the early, middle and late period, the emphasis is differently placed. Diverse 'production planes' determine the particular formulation; first the portrayal of structures of formative forces through the medium of the line (see 'Line and Movement'), then the creation out of the element of colour (see 'From Line to Surface'), and then the reproduction of illustrative-objective memory pictures (see 'From Symbol to Illustration').

The 'dwelling' is inhabited step by step. To start with, the child is hardly open to outside influence in his drawings. His 'gaze' is entirely inwards. Life processes and organ-forming processes determine what he has to say. The next step into the middle phase leads to the walls being broken through. The first orientation towards the outside follows. Doors and windows are opened and light shines into the dwelling. Colour floods in with the light and ensouls the inner space. The regulating element of the late phase is born out of the criteria of external observation.

The drawings teach us to see the development of the child as a process of manifold metamorphoses. Within a continuing process we observe forward leaps, a retarding marking of time or even regressive elements. Looking at the particular stage of development in conjunction with the drawings of particular children the door opens to the understanding of the individuality of the child. The mysteries unravel and we begin to decipher the *hieroglyphs*. Children's drawings make visible the path of incarnation.

Notes on the Study of Man
Wolfgang Schad

It was in the year 1902 that the cave paintings from the end of the last Ice Age, which had been discovered for the first time in Spain thirteen years earlier, were recognized by prehistoric research. Only a few years after that, in 1910, the Russian painter Vassily Kandinsky painted the first abstract picture in Munich. Humanity's oldest and newest painting met across 20,000 years. Contemporaries were at a loss at the time. Altamira was considered a forgery to start with as it had a completely modern effect. And Kandinsky? Was that still art? Was that not much too primitive? Both events brought forms of art into the public eye that did not merely present copies but touched on the sources of the artistic process.

In 1905, between these two occurrences, the Swedish woman, Ellen Key, declared the dawning century to be the century of the child. And one immediately discovered children's paintings to be works of art too, things which had been overlooked for thousands of years, and yet had been produced around us daily in the same way on all continents. It is only more recently that we have begun to judge this third new element that has been brought into public consciousness. Although the Englishman Ebenezer Cooke was probably the first person to occupy himself with children's drawings (as early as 1885), a real interest and the first exhibitions of children's drawings did not come about until after the turn of the 20th century.

Rudolf Steiner founded an anthroposophical science of man at the same time, which is just as new. And this gives us paths of training and a basis for scientific judgment with which we can, in all humility, approach children's drawings through an understanding of the nature of man as a whole. As already mentioned at the beginning of this book, it soon became clear to Hanns Strauss that an aesthetic standard, whatever one understands by that, is not sufficient. The most diverse new directions in art certainly explained children's art to their confederates, praised that part of it which confirmed what they saw in it and evaluated it accordingly. But the child is thus included in adult aesthetics with their minimum claim to art, without being asked. Children do not exhibit. The deed of creation is everything, and fame doesn't concern them. Is it nature; is it soul that appears on the paper?

The present book gives a living answer to these questions. The abundance of material used shows time sequences, which, despite the versatility of the pictures, and despite all the appreciation of each single, unmistakable child-individuality, also have a hidden connection with the child's bodily development. Let us follow up this connection with a few notes on the Study of Man.

Man is a being of many parts. But that does not tell us what holds body and soul together. If we call scientific analysis to our aid, with all its exactness, we know at present only that bio-chemical investigation does not discover any soul, and that psychic introspection does not learn anything about the natural side of man. So the bridge cannot be found either in the physical or psychological realm, but in a realm that belongs to neither of them; namely in the unconscious life processes that both day and night take their course on a sleeping level, in the actual realm of physiology. This has the methodical disadvantage that it cannot be experienced with ordinary day-consciousness either by means of external observation which objectifies or by means of inner feeling which subjectifies. The reason why the bridge is so difficult to know about is because the stronger the life processes are the more unconsciously they function.

But little children paint on this bridge, and everything that they paint takes place from this bridge. Their pictures possess the methodical advantage that they unintentionally show us how this bridge is built, with its individual as well as its typical characteristics. Their scribbles and blobs are the daily by-products of the most important achievements of these years: to be able to grow and gradually bring all the organs to their first stage of maturity. The soul-spiritual nature of small children is primarily engaged in the process of bodily incarnation. They build the bridges of life between body and soul. In their diagrammatic pictures, that which is engaged in building the body rises to the surface of visibility. They are, as it were, the sand washed up out of the ocean of organ-formation, out of the subjectless and objectless 'No-Man's-Land' of life processes. We adults, who have finished growing and have replaced this activity with other activi-ties, have to reorientate ourselves thoroughly, in order to have any understanding whatsoever of that which only intrigues us as yet.

In his earliest pedagogical writings (1907) Rudolf Steiner explains that at the time of so-called birth only the physical, material body becomes separated from the mother. The mobile life structure of the child, however, passes through a further stage of embryonic development lasting for many years. The development of the soul and the freeing of the spirit are further 'births' that prolong human development to about twenty years, which is not the case with any of nature's other creatures.

The life functions that gradually come into play are not, for instance, secured within the body from birth, but are only ready to be developed according to the life conditions encountered. The present-day science of heredity formulates these facets to the effect that neither a bodily characteristic nor the performance of any function is inherited by birth but only mobile norms to react to the particular environment with specific formations and performances; only 'reaction norms' are inherited (A. Kühn 1986). So heredity is the readiness to accept the environment in a specific way. Therefore health characteristics, for instance, are not inherited but only the readiness to develop them if the right conditions are forthcoming. So after birth, too, the child's development consists in being able to unfold, in suitable surroundings, more in the way of health than is there at the beginning. Not until the child has reached school age has the state of health developed to such an extent that basic organic processes have become sufficiently stabilized that they will more or less last a lifetime. This is actually what reaching school-age means. A further reduction of biological dependence, a second birth, takes place at this time. Rudolf Steiner speaks in this sense of a second body becoming free, the life body or etheric body. Infancy is the time when this health body goes through its embryonic development.

If, during the course of its seven years, this second, more delicate pregnancy miscarries, it is a case of embryopathy of the etheric body as, for instance, in a specially crass form in institutionalization. It is a severe retardation of development, which cannot be made up for later, despite good therapeutic physical care in crèches, homes and hospitals, if human unkindness like, say, a repeated change of foster mother prevents the child from forming a consistent soul attachment. Even though there is proper physical care, the lack of a mother or her equivalent, especially during the first three years, leads to severe damage of the life-bearing organization in the child (Schmalohr 1988).

In the first seven years, in their manifestations and especially in their drawings, all children make autobiographical documents which show how this second embryonic development is proceeding. What do they usually paint? Head-and-feet men, vertebral column ladders, broomstick hands; and even the house still has eyes as windows and is the child's own bodily abode. Children, they themselves, as human beings, their bodily activity, their existence through and in the body – or whatever else one should call it – is the theme which ranks higher than anything else if only from the quantitative point of view (Pikunas 1961). Probably there is hardly any-

thing so instructive regarding what is happening in early childhood as this demonstration of the actual, invisible process pouring straight out of the organism in an abundance of scribbles, drawings and coloured paintings. Through their work children unconsciously answer the questions we have raised, if we allow ourselves to go along with them. Everyday matters are festive enough to them. What does *this* picture tell us; what does *that* one?

The earliest drawings, the archetypal whirls, flow from the movement of the little circling hand in an uncontrolled manner, as tracks of living movement. Rocking movements of the hands bring about scribbled pendulum-swings (page 22). Here too, mere thoughts are not sufficient. The wrist construction and degree of muscular development in arms and hands obviously play a part in the character of the forms but they are not the cause of them, for then one could just as well ask what causes the organs to be like they are. And this is just where one comes across the life process that both constructs the bodily organs and creates the pictures that we see. Both arise from the same process. We get to know it. It all happens very quickly and the child loses interest as soon as it has done it. A fragment of anonymous force flows right through the child. We will pass over the quantity of variations that occur throughout the second and third year amongst which significant forms are achieved quite early.

The middle or the end of the third year is decisive. Let us make clear to ourselves once more what happens when the little fellow stands at his small table breathing deeply, and clumsily draws a curved line on the paper; with all the concentration of which a child is capable he tries – how-ever dented it gets – to join the line to its starting point, to close the circle. A big sigh of relief announces that he has achieved it to his complete satisfaction. An enclosed space has been singled out from the vast world, not accidentally, but with intention and understanding. Time and time again the child seeks out and finds the operation as a confirmation. For days at a time lots of pages are scratched all over; the pressure on the paper is often very heavy. It is also the time when children first say 'I' meaningfully. The children discover themselves to be something that does not exist anywhere else in the same way and that now faces the whole world around them. The children have been spiritually continuous ego beings for a long time already but they do not become conscious of it until now.

This achievement of consciousness runs parallel with the increasing maturity of the cerebrum, especially with the development of the medullary sheaths in the cerebral cortex (Wiesener 1964), and with important bone occlusions on the skull. Whilst the fontanels finally close up at the end of the first year, the anterior seam (sutura frontalis = metopica) of the two-and-a-half to three-year-old child now unites between the two frontal bones (Starck 1955) and becomes invisible under X-ray, so that from now on there is one single frontal bone, a dam towards the outside and the inside. The little child's cosmically-open consciousness that used to identify itself with its surroundings everywhere where it felt protected and which, up till now, we could experience outside the little body more than within it, withdraws at this point behind the frontal bone that is closing up. The first phase of defiance begins.

Children want to close themselves off and so this is also produced in drawing. 'I have shut it', the child says, commenting on the joined-up circle on the paper.

Hollow forms and spirals as well as circles and crosses make up the material that is now used to experience and complete the new mystery within. At the same time the straight line now begins to assert itself more and more. Between the third and the end of the fifth year it is increasingly used as an axis of symmetry. The motif grows into a square, a rectangle, into repetitions of the same or similar lines in rhythmic succession. Towers are built, or rather ladders or networks of steps. Children paint the functional maturing of their vertebral column, that towering pillar of drums that is symmetrically accompanied by ganglions, blood-vessel ladders, groups of muscles and steps of ribs.

Physiologically the rib-cage breathing or, to be more exact, the rib breathing is now superimposed on the diaphragm breathing which predominated up to the third year. The round, barrel-shaped rib cage of the baby flattens out in front now and it has a wider diameter sideways (Rauper-Kopsch 2003). The vertebra unites with the body of the sternum so the most rhythmic part of the skeleton, the vertebral column, assumes its finished form. Thus in this middle stage of early childhood the whole rhythmic system of the body is developing.

More than ever before the children now choose and enjoy swinging and rocking toys, all kinds of round games, the refrain of songs and hearing the same stories over and over again. In fact, regular rhythms throughout the day, in the course of the week and during the year, so that everything becomes an unquestioned ritual as far as possible, show that children require routine in order to build up and stabilize their own biological rhythm, their 'inner clock'. Their bodily health for life depends on this; indeed it is a further contribution to the capacity for health that mediates between body and soul. Expectation is satisfied – it happened before, it is happening now, and I can rely on it happening again – supplies a basic trust in life, gives the necessary ballast. The pictures drawn between two and a half and five, in particular, give an account of the development of this rhythmic health organism.

At this time, especially during the fifth year – that is, the four-year-olds – draw head-and-feet men with a lot of very long sense-threads reaching out and creating strong connections with everything that is now 'environment'. These antennae are obviously not just hair, but we see a presence of life coming into the picture, which has a strong hold on the child. We would like to enlarge a little on this.

By now it has become general knowledge that the human being is not limited to five senses but has several others as well, like organs for sensing warmth and cold, and others in the inner ear for perceiving gravity and movement, etc. Free nerve endings in most of the organs give us perceptions of our own state of health, pain or bodily well being, hunger or satisfaction, tiredness or freshness. Rudolf Steiner summed up these latter sensations as the 'sense of life'. Now, with little children, we can observe that there is something peculiar about their sense of life. They often cannot properly localize bodily pain as yet. She has hurt her knee and says she has a tummy ache. And if you ask more precisely, 'Where?' then she points to the barbed wire outside. They can localize happenings in their surroundings much better that in their own small bodies. It is the sense of life in particular that is still to a large extent directed towards the life of the surroundings. As a grown-up it is difficult to recall how very differently one experienced things as a four-year-old, as though wandering in a dream; the gooseberry bushes in the garden; the cool early autumn morning with the first conkers under the tree; the road, the edge of the neighbouring wood … the presence or absence of life was still felt much more keenly.

When children reach school age the sense of life reorientates itself; it looks inwards towards the child's own body. This reversal is completed by puberty. If we return as grown-ups to the place of our early childhood we are often surprised and disappointed by its ordinary everyday-ness. After the sense of life has adjusted itself to the life processes within the body, then our surroundings become void of life. But the cause of this is not out there but in our altered sense-organism. What we have touched on here concerning one sense realm of the small child, applies to a whole number of other areas of the senses as well; the conditions in the surrounding world are sensed much more strongly psychologically than their own body is. This is what makes children imitative beings, and this comes into the picture with the antennae-covered head-and-feet men we see at this age (pages 59 to 60).

In the drawing done by the child who is just five (page 61), we are surprised by the 'steering-wheel' in the tummy area of the manikin. What was previously rayed out by the whole manikin becomes restricted by the body, begins for the first time to turn towards the body. It is not difficult to identify this wheel with the solar plexus, a part of the vegetative nervous system in the upper abdominal cavity. All its parts supply the unconsciously working organs that are withdrawn from our own volition, as are most of those within the abdominal cavity. This nervous system is distinguished anatomically from the other nerves, which are more consciously at the disposal of the soul, by two characteristics; the vegetative nerves form a loosely woven network (plexus), with no clear centre. On the other hand a massive concentration in the nervous organism is situated in the spinal cord and especially in the brain, which is why one contrasts the 'animal' or central nervous system with the 'vegetative' nervous system.

The other characteristic of the latter is that fatty sheaths, the so-called medullary sheaths, do not cover the nerves. Non-medullated nerve fibres work principally below the conscious level as distinct from our day consciousness, which is based on medullated nerves. In the realm of the former the processes of recuperation and growth, which work in a perpetual sleeping state, take place by coordinating the organs one with another and building up order in the life structure. We also try to create order with the help of the central nervous system, but this is quite a different kind of order, namely order in the consciousness.

Now we have to realize that the central nervous system, too, is originally non-medullated. That is, the soul is asleep to begin with for the whole body in the way it is later on for the vegetative organs. Up till this time, however, the future central nervous system is doing most of its growing. To begin with it is, from a functional point of view, really engaged in vegetative activity; actually it is the first centre of metabolism in the embryonic and infant stage. And the vegetative functions are only gradually taken over by the trunk and especially the abdominal organism.

Compared to the vast number of questions that can be raised, very little is known up to the present about the bodily development of the small child. It is understandable that research was concerned in the first place with the ill child. Pediatry (knowledge of child medicine) has been developed but pedology (knowledge of children) has only just begun. However, regarding our questions about the connection between the child's bodily and artistic activity, we can obtain a certain amount of help from a recent work on the nervous system. Following suggestions made by Steiner (1919, 1925) Rohen for the first time in 1971 pointed out that the kind of formations, forms and functions of the nerve organization are more readily understood if one replaces the old division into two parts by a division into three parts; into brain (sensorium), spinal cord (senso-motory) and, as before, the intestinal nervous system (vegetativum). We have already seen that these three realms do not mature absolutely simultaneously but one after the other. The brain reaches a clear stage in the third year. The stabilizing of the rhythmic and motor activities between the third and fifth birthday indicates the functional maturity of the spinal cord. Not until then are the vegetative nerve functions increasingly taken over by the intestinal nervous system. After the fifth year this becomes completely independent of the centralized nervous system, and just at this age it comes more and more into the picture as an autonomous system. It now 'steers' itself.

An insight into the space-time formation of the whole of bodily development is also important for the understanding of children's drawings. Let us go a long way back and take a look at the embryonic development of the physical body. A marked heterochrony, a 'difference in timing', strikes us at once. In the sixth week the central nervous system is way ahead of the development of the other organs; the brain does not only take up the largest part of the head but it is also as big as the whole trunk. The spinal cord is so long that the end of it is not yet overgrown by the loin and pelvis area and so the point protrudes below, without having anything to do with the tail of an animal, which always grows out behind the future pelvic area (Blechschmidt 1968). In the twelfth week we clearly find the rib-cage area growing rapidly. It catches up with the head, as it were, whilst the abdominal area is still very small. And the abdominal organs and the limbs do not grow in proportion until later. From the first to the seventh year, in the period of the life-body's pregnancy, which is less striking that the physical one yet so much easier to observe, we have the same 'difference in timing'. Up to the third year functional development takes place first in the region of the head, then up to the fifth year predominantly in the upper region of the trunk, and not until then does the equivalent development start up in the region of the metabolism and the limbs; and this is where the main growth is then, although it takes place over the whole organism where change of matter and muscle activity occur (Steiner 1921).

So beginning in the sixth year and progressing

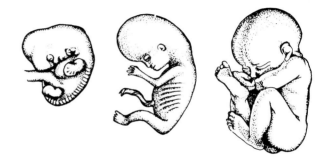

Heterochrony of embryonic growth of organs of the physical body scaled to equal head size for comparison: 6th week (1 cm), 11th week (6 cm), fully developed (30 cm head to buttocks)

more rapidly in the seventh, the limbs catch up on the slow start they made in their development in infancy. An increase in growth can begin in the feet and hands, soon continuing into the arms and legs. The form of the trunk changes conspicuously too. The small child's potbelly disappears so that there is a waist for the first time. The covering of fat is generally reduced with the intensified metabolism and the shape of the muscles as well as of the joints are more pronounced. The whole form becomes slimmer; the shape of the rib cage, which was originally an obtuse angle, now becomes acute and the neck grows longer and stronger. When these processes take hold of the head the physiognomy changes, so that the rounded forehead becomes flatter and no longer arches above the face. Instead of this the mouth part grows stronger, making room in the jaws for the coming second teeth, so that this part of the face now comes to the fore for the first time. In this last stage of infancy, through changes in matter and shape, children create for themselves a new form of existence (first organic change, see Zeller 1964).

Children record this process too, in their drawings of this age as in a snapshot. The head-and-feet men they have been drawing do not usually acquire their first neck and trunk until now. And these 'trunk-and-feet' men often have especially long legs, feet, arms and hands, and gigantic fingers. All the houses with doors and windows, roof and chimney, with people looking out or visibly going about their business inside, arise out of the change in the children's bodily experience. The children are more contained because they move into their 'house' and look out. From this position they also increasingly paint what one cannot be all by oneself; large numbers of 'picture-stories' appear. Pictures turn more and more into scenes. What is particularly interesting is that the children only now fully discover colour. If it was largely used as a contrast to the background before, now it is used for its own sake. Inner warmth of colour lights up which is obviously experienced in itself.

On the other hand contours get sharper. The line is no longer a line of movement but a boundary between what is inside and what is outside. As children's bodies grow more slender it is the angularity that they now experience most, and this leads to the popular and much-used triangular figure. It contains the elements of a firm basis and purposeful striving. The acute angles predominate – that is, not those which ray out but those into which something is received. The triangle dominates this age (pages 80, 81 and 82).

On page 82 we were told that it is often noticed that children draw fewer pictures during the end of infancy, roughly between the sixth and the end of the seventh year. Their overflowing liveliness ebbs somewhat. Children acquire more the position of observers of their environment than of the active portrayers that they used to be. They tend towards apathy. Psychologists that do not understand the body assume that stimuli are lacking in the kindergarten or home setting. But the causes are different ones and they are justified. Namely, the children are engaged in a very exacting task. They are working at the rapid rebuilding of their bodily form. This is no automatic material process but one that can be seen to happen with an expenditure of energy that is drawn from imaginative soul activity.

The first organic change and preparation for the change of teeth is an unstable time. Even energetic games are cut down. The heartbeat is irregular at times (respiratory arrhythmy) and this only occurs otherwise during the second organic change at puberty (Wiesener 1964). Psychic anomalies are more frequently observed (Pavloff 1950). Susceptibility to infection increases at times. The passage to new shores is an inharmonious period. This pause in outer artistic activity is indeed no pause in the functional development of the bodily-orientated life processes, which now have to complete their own 'embryonic stage'. Clearly the springboard is being built in, with which to be able to leap into the middle of childhood with its different kind of faculty for learning and for imagination and play. Whatever alien demands are made on the body, namely school learning at too early an age, however attractive it is made for children, will undermine basic confidence, the unconscious trust in existence, for the rest of the child's life.

As is shown in the diagram, the formation of

the tooth crowns of both the milk teeth and the permanent teeth are finished by the time the child is seven; only the wisdom teeth are an exception to this, for they lag behind. In the case of the second teeth, it was during the kindergarten years that the hardest top layers, the enamel covering on the permanent teeth, were built behind the gums. Apart from the wisdom teeth, the school age child has completed this formation of the hardest substance in the body. Just the roots of the teeth, composed of softer tooth bone (dentine), are still to come. What is now finished in the way of the perfecting of the body and the stabilizing of the functions in all the three systems described, is in the form of surplus energy at the disposal of learning. The capacity for independently experienced thought, memory, imagination and intelligence becomes free. School age has been attained.

So the forces that children previously used for growing and developing are the very same that they also used all the time for scribbling, drawing and painting. From now on the forces of growth that have become more independent of the body will be used so that through playing they can work and through working they can learn.

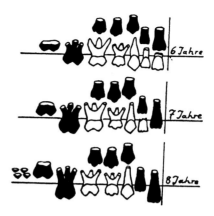

Development of dentition at early school age. The diagram shows the right half of the upper jaw; vertical line indicates middle of jaw; horizontal line the level of the gum; milk teeth are shown white and permanent teeth black.
The first visible sign of the change of teeth occurs in the six-year-old with the appearance of the first additional molar. In the seven-year-old the first incisor has changed. (Actually the sequence is frequently reversed nowadays.) In the eight-year-old the first calcification of the last molar (wisdom tooth) commences with the four points of the crown. Note the stage of development of the crowns of the permanent teeth in the seven-year-old.

Bibliography

Aeppli, Willi: The Care and Development of the Human Senses. Steiner Schools Fellowship in Great Britain 1993.

Biechschmidt, Erich: Vom Ei zum Embryo. Stuttgart 1968.

Britsch, Gustav: Theorie der bildenden Kunst. Egon Kornmann (ed.), Munich 1926.

Cooke, Ebenezer: Art Teaching and Child Nature. Journal of Education, London 1885.

Geiger, Rudolf: Mit Märchen im Gespräch. Stuttgart 1972.

Giedion, S.: Die Entstehung der Kunst. Cologne 1964.

Gollwitzer, Gerhard: Schule des Sehens. Ravensburg 1960.

Grözinger, Wolfgang: Kinder kritzeln, zeichnen, malen. Munich 1952.

Hartlaub, G. F.: Der Genius im Kinde. Breslau 1930.

Heymann, Karl: Kind und Kunst. Journal: Psychologische Praxis, No. 10, Basel 1951.

Key, Ellen: Das Jahrhundert des Kindes. Berlin 1902.

Kienzle, Richard: Das bildhafte Gestalten. Esslingen 1932.

König, Karl: The First Three Years of the Child. Anthroposophic Press, New York 1969.

Koch, Karl: Der Baumtest. Bern/Stuttgart 1967.

Koch, Rudolf: Das Zeichenbuch. Leipzig 1936.

Kressler, Erika: Die kindliche Entwicklung im ersten Jahrsiebt und ihre Ausdrucksformen beim gesunden und behinderten Kind. Journal: Menschenschule, Vol. 50, No. 4, Basel.

Kühn, Alfred: Grundriss der Vererbungslehre. 9th ed. Heidelberg 1986.

Kühn, Herbert: Eiszeitkunst, die Geschichte ihrer Erforschung. Göttingen 1965.

Lenz, Friedel: Bildsprache der Märchen. 8th ed. Stuttgart 1997.

Lusseyran, Jacques: The Blind in Society and Blindness, A New Seeing of the World. The Myrin Institute, New York 1973.

Meyer, Rudolf: Die Weisheit der deutschen Volksmärchen. 8th ed. Stuttgart 1981.

Meyers, Hans: Die Welt der kindlichen Bildnerei. Witten 1957.

Morris, Desmond: Biology of Art: A Study of the Picture-making Behaviour of the Great Apes and its Relationship to Human Art. Methuen, London 1962.

Pavloff, Th.: Ueber das gehäufte Auftreten psychischer Auffälligkeiten in der Zeit des ersten Gestaltwandels beim Kinde. Journal: Kinderärztliche Praxis. Vol. 18. No. 7/8 (1950).

Pikunas, J. and H. Carberry: Standardization of the Graphoscopic Scale: The Content of Children's Drawings. Journal of Clinical Psychology, Vol. 17 (1961).

Rauber, A. and Fr. Kopsch: Lehrbuch und Atlas der Anatomie, Vol. 1. 3rd rev. ed. Stuttgart 2003.

Rohen, Johannes: Funktionelle Neuroanatomie, Lehrbuch u. Atlas. 6th rev. ed. Stuttgart and New York 2001.

Schad, Wolfgang: Das Kind im Sog der Zivilisation. Journal: Die Kommenden, Vol. 27, No. 2, Freiburg 1973.

Schmalohr, Emil: Frühe Mutterentbehrung bei Mensch und Tier. Entwicklungspsychologische Studie zur Psychohygiene der frühen Kindheit. Munich/Basel 1968.

Schuchhardt, Wolfgang: Das kindliche Zeichnen. Journal: Erziehungskunst, Vol. 21, No. 4, Stuttgart 1957.

Schwenk, Theodor: Sensitive Chaos. The Creation of Flowing Forms in Water and Air. Rudolf Steiner Press. London 1976.

Sembdner, Helmut: Hanns Strauss als Interpret kindlicher Zeichenkunst. Journal: Erziehungskunst, Vol. 16, No. 5/6, Stuttgart 1952.

Steiner, Rudolf: Study of Man. Rudolf Steiner Press, London 1975

– Die gesunde Entwicklung des Leiblich-Physischen als Grundlage der freien Entfaltung des Seelisch-Geistigen (7th lecture). Dornach 1969.

– The Education of the Child. Rudolf Steiner Press, London 1975.

– Occult Science – An Outline. Rudolf Steiner Press, London 1972.

– The Spritual Guidance of Man. Anthroposophic Press, New York 1977.

– An Occult Physiology. Rudolf Steiner Publishing Company, London 1951.

– Theosophy. Rudolf Steiner Press, London 1973.

Steiner, Rudolf and Ita Wegman: Extending Practical Medicine. Rudolf Steiner Press, London 1996.

Strauss, Hanns: Die Gestaltungskraft des Kleinkindes als Offenbarer seines Wesens. Journal: Erziehungskunst, Vol. 6, No. 4, Stuttgart 1932.

– Die Bedeutung des Zeichnens für das Kleinkind. Journal: Erziehungskunst, Vol. 16, No. 5/6, Stuttgart 1952.

Strauss, Michaela: Analyse einer Kinderzeichnung. Nach Aufzeichnungen von Hanns Strauss. Journal: Erziehungskunst, Vol. 22, No. 1/2, Stuttgart 1958.

– Was offenbaren uns die Kleinkinderzeichnungen? Journal: Erziehungskunst, Vol. 33, No. 5/6, Stuttgart 1969.

– Wie frühkindliches Malen und Zeichnen in der Schule verwandelt wird. Journal: Erziehungskunst, Vol. 33, No. 8/9, Stuttgart 1969.

Trümper, Herbert: Malen und Zeichnen in Kindheit und Jugend. Vol. III, Berlin 1961.

Vogel, Lothar: Der dreigliedrige Mensch. Dornach 1967.

Wiesener, Heinrich (ed.): Einführung in die Entwicklungsphysiologie des Kindes. Heidelberg, Berlin, New York 1964.

Wildlöcher, Daniel: Was eine Kinderzeichnung verrät. Jochen Stork (ed.), Munich 1974.

Zeller, Wilfried: Konstitution und Entwicklung. Göttingen 1964.

Related Books on Education, Child Development and Curative Education

by Rudolf Steiner:

The Study of Man

Practical Advice to Teachers

Discussions with Teachers

Education as a Social Problem

The Kingdom of Childhood

Human Values in Education

The Four Temperaments

The Education of the Child in the Light of Anthroposophy

Education for Special Needs

by other authors:

The Way of a Child, A. C. Harwood

The Recovery of Man in Childhood, A. C. Harwood

Portrait of a Waldorf School, A. C. Harwood

Rudolf Steiner's Gift to Education. The Waldorf Schools, L. F. Edmunds

The Scientific and the Moral in Education, L. F. Edmunds

Education Towards Freedom, F. Carlgren

Observation, Thinking, The Senses, E. Hutchins

The Care and Development of the Human Senses, W. Aeppli

The Experience of Knowledge. Essays on American Education, J. F. Gardner

Respect for Life. The Traditional Upbinging of American Indian Children, S. M. Morey & O. Gilliam

Childhood. A Study of the Growing Soul, C. von Heydebrand

The Curriculum of the First Waldorf Schools, E. A. K. Stockmeyer

Form Drawing, H. R. Niederhäuser & M. Frohlich

Dynamic Drawing. Its Therapeutic Aspects, H. Kirchner

Geometric Drawing and the Waldorf School Plan, H. von Baravalle

Introduction to Physics in the Waldorf Schools, H. von Baravalle

The Teaching of Arithmetic and the Waldorf School Plan, H. von Baravalle

Early Childhood Education and the Waldorf School Plan, E. M. Grunelius

Teaching Children to Write, A. E. McAllen

Questions and Answers on Rudolf Steiner Education, R. Wilkinson

A Child is Born. Pregnancy, Birth and First Childhood, W. zur Linden, M.D.

An Introduction to Anthroposophical Medicine, V. Bott, M.D.

Healing Education Based on Anthroposophy's Image of Man, ed. B. Fischer